Win it for....

What a World Championship Means to Generations of Red Sox Fans

by
Sons of Sam Horn

www.sonsofsamhorn.com

Foreword by
Curt Schilling

www.SportsPublishingLLC.com

ISBN: 1-59670-084-X

All photos courtesy of the individual writer of the corresponding Win it for.... post.

Publishers: Peter L. Bannon and Joseph J. Bannon Sr.
Senior managing editor: Susan M. Moyer
Acquisitions editor: Dean Miller
Developmental editors: Dean Miller and Elisa Bock Laird
Art director: K. Jeffrey Higgerson
Dust jacket design: Kenneth J. O'Brien
Project manager: Kenneth J. O'Brien
Imaging: Kenneth J. O'Brien
Photo editor: Erin Linden-Levy
Vice president of sales and marketing: Kevin King
Media and promotions managers: Courtney Hainline (regional),
	Randy Fouts (national), Maurey Williamson (print)

Printed in the United States of America

Sports Publishing L.L.C.
804 North Neil Street
Champaign, IL 61820

Phone: 1-877-424-2665
Fax: 217-363-2073
Web site: www.SportsPublishingLLC.com

To Red Sox fans everywhere and to those who suffer from cancer or ALS.

In the spirit of the Win It For.... thread, a large portion of the author proceeds from the sale of this book is being donated to the Dana Farber Cancer Institute and Curt's Pitch for ALS.

Foreword

Have you ever run across someone who just "gets it"? Someone who has a different take on things, a perspective that others might pass off or snicker at, but when all is said and done, it's blatantly obvious they get it? I firmly believe when you turn the last page of this book you will understand that the Red Sox Nation "gets it."

I have been asked to write this foreword, I think, because in some small way I think I am one of these people, a SoSH'er, albeit one looking at this compilation from the other side of the glass.

I became a member of SoSH sometime around Thanksgiving in 2003. During that time I was negotiating with the Boston Red Sox on what would eventually turn out to be a three-year contract that, God willing, will see me end my career as a member of the Sox. I can't even remember who it was that sent me an email one night that week, alerting me to a website called "The Sons of Sam Horn." The only thing I was told was that it was a fanatic and devout group of Sox fans and that I might be interested to get their perspective on what was happening with regard to my current situation.

Well fast forward a year or so, and here we are. After riding what could only be described as a once-in-a-lifetime roller coaster, the Sox are World Champs, and Red Sox Nation breathes a little easier these days, walks a little lighter, and looks at its hometown boys a little differently.

Let's be very clear, Red Sox baseball IS a religion; there can be no questioning that. Being a member of the Nation is a privilege, a right of passage, an inheritance. Now I don't say this as if it's something I've always known, because I haven't. These things can only be understood by Sox fans, and the people in the Sox organizations. That's not to say other teams in other sports don't have an awesome relationship, there are many and they are varied. Rabid Raiders fans, Chiefs fans, Steeler fans, Yankee fans, the Dog Pound in

Cleveland, Bleacher bums in Wrigley, St Louis and their incredible set of devoted and smart Cardinal fans, Packer fans, and on and on. But having grown up an enormous sports fan myself, and watched them all, experienced a lot of them, I can't fathom a more devout and loyal group of people than the ones who proclaim themselves members of Red Sox Nation. Other than the Cubs, it might be the only group of fans on the planet that has had the rest of the world rooting for them time and time again, only to see their hopes and fears dashed by a light-hitting shortstop's 300-foot homer, a routine ground ball, a wild pitch, and so many other little plays that only added to the 86 years of accumulated frustration.

But the Red Sox have one thing no other team in sports has, one thing that makes them unique, makes their story different than everyone else's— they have a villain, and that villain's name is the New York Yankees. The Yankess have long been sport's gold standard, and rightly so. Twenty-six world titles in less than a century will endear you to no one outside your loyal fan base. Mr Steinbrenner might be verbally attacked more than any owner in sports. From my perspective it's something I have never understood. A team's owner chooses to spend enormous amounts of his revenue on his TEAM, what a concept. An owner willing to do anything, ANYTHING, to win a World Series. Every team in every sport should be so lucky. Not only does he sign most of the game's best free agents, but most of those players are champions in their own right. Jeter, Posada, Williams, O'Neill, Pettite, Sheffield, Martinez, Riveras, and on and on. Guys that you revel in competing against because even though their stats might not make people think they are the very best in the game, you know as a player that beating them means beating the BEST. They are winners, champions, their ultimate goal is to get the ring, regardless of what the stat sheets say.

An owner with bottomless pockets, a team with championship players, a fan base of incredibly smart, incredibly vulgar, and incredibly passionate people. If you aren't a Yankee fan, what's to like? If you are a Red Sox fan what's not to despise? You have a similar storied history, a resume of Hall of Fame players, a tremendous run of tradition, yet you have no ring. At every turn, every season, almost every single bad memory in Sox history the Yankees are somewhere to be found. Oh, the agony.

Now we come full circle. The book you hold is a compilation of letters written by members of Red Sox Nation, and in it as you will see, they get it. They understand that in a day and age of greed, unfathomable salaries, pampered athletes, spoiled owners, horribly slanderous and out-of-control sports media, steroids, drugs, crime, and all the other negative focal points people love to wallow in, that, in the end, it comes down to your TEAM.

It's not about who's signing where for how much, who is mad at whom, what this guy said about that guy, why the hell does the manager do this, and that, why doesn't he do this, and that, this guy sucks, this guy's overpaid, this guy's underpaid, he's nice, he's a jerk, trade him, trade for them, release this guy, sign that guy. Oh, those things matter to Sox fans, but in the end they really didn't. Sox fans are the most scrutinizing bunch of people on the planet. They can tell you my ERA and OPS against between pitches 57-62, in day games, vs AL West opponents, in odd months. But when all was said and done, when Foulkie flipped the now infamous baseball to Doug at first base, and the Boston Red Sox were crowned World Series Champions for the first time in pretty much every one of our lives, you had this book. You had the people who had lived, died, went to sleep and woke up with the red "B" on their brains, thoughts and feelings on just what this whole thing really means to true fans. What it really is all about to people that care so much for their hometown team it hurts.

As a player I can tell you that it took me some time, even now I am not sure I totally understand it, to get it. To understand what this really and truly meant to members of Red Sox nation. I can remember a ton of instances during the October run when Kevin Millar or Doug Mirabelli and I would be talking about winning it all. The one thing we kept coming back to was "What will these people do if we do win it?," "What does this all really mean to them?"

Well those two questions are answered time and time again in this book. I can tell you as a player that it was an honor to have been part of something so special to so many, something no one will ever take away from the 25 guys who won eight straight games in unprecedented fashion. That became the first team ever to come back and win it all down three games to none, against the Yankees no less.

What a run, what a year, enjoy the book.

God Bless,
Curt Schilling

Preface

It all started because of a word that had been often used in countless threads on a Red Sox Internet message board called "Sons of Sam Horn."

Mojo.

Mojo, according to *Webster's Dictionary*, is a noun with an intriguing denotation: "A magic power or supernatural spell."

After the last out of Game 3 of the 2004 American League Championship Series, nearly every member of SoSH—some 1,900 strong—had called upon whatever mojo they could muster to help their beloved Red Sox stave off the shackles of elimination against the hated New York Yankees. From the inclusion of the complete text of Act IV, Scene 3 of Shakespeare's *Henry V* ("We few, we happy few . . .") to the publication of a series of montages depicting heroic players from Boston's sports past, nearly every poster beseeched the gods on behalf of their beloved team.

As a Sox fan who had followed the team on a pitch-by-pitch basis since 1963, I had experienced enough Red Sox pathos to turn me into the ultimate oxymoron—a raging existentialist. Still, as the 2004 playoffs unfolded, I, like countless other Red Sox fans, didn't allow myself to wallow in abject misery this time. I even went on a local New York radio station after Game 3 of the ALCS and proclaimed, "Listen, there has never been a curse. If we can somehow win Game 4, the Yankees will be in trouble. You watch."

William Jennings Bryan once wrote, "Destiny is not a matter of chance, it is a matter of choice. It is not a thing to be waited for; it is a thing to be achieved." I wore a Red Sox hat to work each day that week. I believed.

And—incredibly—the Red Sox miraculously tied up the 2004 ALCS with a trio of exhausting victories over their archrivals, two of them in extra innings.

On the morning of the seventh game, October 20, I sat down at my teacher's desk and began pounding away on my computer keyboard during a free period, crafting my own particular mojo that—I hoped—would ultimately defeat the despised Yankees. I called it, "Win It For."

"Win it for Johnny Pesky, who deserves to wear a Red Sox uniform in the dugout during the 2004 World Series," I began. "Win it for Bobby Doerr, who, through the sadness of losing his beloved [wife] Monica, would love to see his Sox finally defeat New York in Yankee Stadium."

I urged them to win it for other Red Sox icons—Dom DiMaggio, Carl Yastrzemski, Ted Williams, Tony Conigliaro. For Red Sox announcers who had helped hone our love for the team before they passed on—Ned Martin, Ken Coleman, Jim Woods.

I urged them to win it for friends, for other SoSH members.

And finally, most of all, I urged them to win it for my own father, James Lawrence Kelly, 1913-1986, who "always told me that loyalty and perseverance go hand in hand. Thanks for sharing the best part of you with me."

As I was writing, I realized there might be others who'd want to dedicate a possible championship to those individuals in their own lives who had loved the Red Sox through thick and thin.

I was right.

From the grateful man who lost his brother in Okinawa 60 years ago, to the sibling who dedicated a Sox victory to her brother who perished on September 11, 2001, there were scores of tributes from the populace of Red Sox Nation, young and old. Each poster added something unique to what became a compelling Red Sox mosaic.

Before the fourth game of the World Series, an old friend e-mailed me: "It is remarkable to me that each and every one of the contributors to the 'Win It For' thread reveal something extraordinary about themselves in the end. That is the enduring miracle found within its pages."

The "Win It For" thread, a small idea in the beginning, became a very big deal in the end. One writer called it, "the Red Sox fan's 'Chicken Soup for the Soul.'" Another compared it to the Vietnam Memorial Wall. When it was finally locked after eight days, more than 1,000 people had added to it. It would be featured in newspapers from Boston to Los Angeles, from Miami to Chicago. Peter Jennings would include it in his nightly news report on ABC. The gang on ESPN's *Baseball Tonight* would mention it during a discourse on Red Sox Nation.

In early November, ten days after the last out of the World Series, I received a note from a most perceptive "lurker" to the website. He wrote: "You know, Shaun, I really believe that the ghosts that we all beckoned, our dearly departed fathers and grandfathers, sisters, brothers, neighbors, coaches, and friends, had a hand in the astonishing two weeks that we've just experienced. In a way, it was their last loving act to us. And we, in turn, responded as only we could . . . in the posts that we ultimately submitted."

The "Win It For" thread is a tribute to a most underrated virtue—loyalty. It is a sonnet to a team that has been a defining obsession for an entire region of people for more than five generations.

As always, the loquacious Kevin Millar nailed it moments after the World Series ended when he exclaimed, "The fans and the players—we did this all . . . together." Mojo indeed.

What follows is a collection of searing and heartfelt postings from hundreds of fans who wanted to dedicate a Red Sox victory to some unforgettable people.

A bit of advice to the reader from one who knows: Settle down in your favorite chair, sit back, and have a box of Kleenex with you. You'll need to have some tissues close by.

—Shaun Kelly

Win it for....

Win it for Johnny Pesky, who deserves to wear a Red Sox uniform in the dugout during the 2004 World Series. Mr. Henry, the trophy needs to be presented first of all to him.

Win it for Bobby Doerr, who, through the sadness of losing his beloved Monica, would love to see his Sox finally defeat New York in Yankee Stadium. Revenge is best served cold.

Win if for Dommie, the most loyal and devoted of men. If he hadn't gotten hurt in Game 7 of the '46 Series, Enos Slaughter would never have scored.

Win it for Carl Yastrzemski. While his heart still aches today, may a smile break through his personal storm-cloud this evening. His beloved son, Mike, will show us the way. God speed, number eight.

Win it for Ted, who once said, "If they ever won it, I would feel so @#%$ warm inside."

Win it for Tony, who taught us all the meaning of courage and grit. A day doesn't go by when I don't think of you, number 25.

Win it for Nedly and Ken and Possum—who provided us with nothing less than the soundtrack to our child-hoods.

Win it for Richard Gorman, who followed the team passionately while residing in Queens and the Bronx. He was a master teacher, a supportive friend, and a diehard Red Sox fan.

Win if for Stiffy—who saw firsthand Denny Galehouse's hanging curves, worshiped the Golden Greek even after he died so suddenly back in '55, and got misty-eyed when Rico Petrocelli began to back-peddle on a squirting pop-up to short left-field on a placid October afternoon back in 1967.

Win if for Cheri—may she cry on Giff's shoulders tonight in pure joy and emotion—and not in the stew of pathos. Cheri's unconditional love for the Red Sox serves as a genuine measuring stick for us all.

Win it for Felix—who began living out "The September of My Years" last month as he hit fifty; a fan who has always believed that the impossible is just not a dream.

Win it for Eric Van. Eric, you have truly embodied Hemingway's definition of courage recently. Grace under pressure, indeed.

Win it for Eric Van's father.

Win it for Dalton and Moose and Norm and Buck and Zup and all of the other old-timers on this board whose lives have defined the virtue of loyalty.

Win it for our far-off posters, from Manila to Montana to Mark in London, who have continually kept the home fires burning thousands of miles away from Route 128.

Most of all, win it for James Lawrence Kelly, 1913-1986. This one's for you, Daddy. You always told me that loyalty and perseverance go hand in hand. Thanks for sharing the best part of you with me.

—Shaun Kelly

Win it for my grandfather, Joseph Francis Burns (1900-1986), who played for the White Sox (not the most prolific entry in the *Baseball Encyclopedia*) and taught me the passion of baseball. He was not a fan of any specific team because he just loved baseball. Any great game. Any great series. Any great comeback. He instilled in me this love of the game. And I am forever grateful.

—Jennifer Burns

Win it for all of us who sat glued to the TV until the wee hours of the morning during the ALCS, with our hearts pounding out of our chests until the final run was scored or the final out was made, knowing we had to get out of bed in a few hours to go to work and being giddy that we got to do it again the next night.

Win it for my wife who both indulges and shares my passion for the Sox, my son watching in his apartment at college in Charlottesville, and my daughter also watching from college in Blacksburg, each enjoying it in their own way, but mainly because they know how much it means to me.

Win it for my dad, who passed his love for the Sox on to me.

—EG in VA

Win it for my father. He was a lifelong Sox fan who grew up idolizing Ted Williams, and raised me on the virtues of the Red Sox as both a fun diversion and as a character building exercise. As the players came and went, he would examine each new arrival with the keen eye of the hard-to-please calculus professor he was, closely scrutinizing the players and then passing judgment on their worthiness to wear the Sox colors. He spent much time praising Nomar and lambasting Mo Vaughn, and he always made me laugh when he called Roger Clemens a "thick-head." He told me Pedro was the best pitcher he ever saw, bar none; greater than Gibson, Seaver, or Koufax in their primes.

He never lived long enough to see them win it all. He passed away unexpectedly in December 1999. The last game we ever watched together was Game 3 of the 1999 ALCS, when Pedro dominated the Yankees and the Sox sent Roger to the shower on a glorious October afternoon.

Here's to you, Dad.

**—Steve Salhany
(Smiling Joe Hesketh)**

Win it for the littlest Red Sox fans. My boys 6/3/2 are all Red Sox fans. I dare to think of raising boys that think of the Red Sox as "winners" who won in 2004.

Win it for all the grandparents from New England who instilled the love of baseball in their grandchildren. My grandfather (from Lee, MA), dad and uncle took me to my first Sox game in 1979. Sadly, my grandfather became ill this past year and passed away in December. I got to meet with him shortly before he passed—and he said, "the Red Sox will win it this year." When Boston was down 3-0 to NY, I thought a loss to NY would let my grandfather down more than me…. there is no team in sport that means nearly as much to its fandom….

**—Mark Sewell
(Soxfanincleveland)
Turnbull, CT**

Win it for my dad (1960-2004) who passed his love for Boston sports on to my brother and me.

**—Ryan Kilcoyne
(SoxScout)**

Win it for my Dad, Richard Anderson Sr. (1945-1994). I was only 9 when my dad died, but the best memories I have from growing up is talking baseball with my dad. He bought weekend season tickets to the Sox in 1987, and we never missed a game. My dad was always happiest watching the Red Sox, and I couldn't help but think of him watching the celebration. I always had a hard time going to the cemetery to visit his grave, it just made it too real for me as a kid. Knowing that the headstone was for my hero, and the greatest man I have ever met, was just too much for me to handle. I am ashamed to say I have not been able to bring myself to visit his grave in about 2 years, but when I come home from college this weekend to attend Games 1 and 2 of the World Series, I am going to make a stop down the cemetery and celebrate with my dad. And I want to thank the Red Sox for that.

—Rick Anderson Jr.

Win it for everyone who was crushed in '46 (and '67, and '75, and '78, and '86, and '03).

Win it for all the fans who put off (and are still putting off) their college applications the week before they're due to watch every moment of every game.

Win it for everyone who never thought it would happen, and who won't believe it has after they do.

Win it for everyone who can't help but grin when the hear "Dirty Water."

Win it for every Red Sox fan who couldn't take it anymore and lost faith, only to come crawling back come playoff time (that one's for you, Jack).

And more importantly than the last one, win it for all the fans who never lost faith. Ever.

Win it now.

It ends tonight.

—Ben Larrison
(fan14bosox)

Win it for my father, Francis Kelly Bell. The man who took me to my first baseball game, August 20, 1983, at Fenway Park. Sox vs. Jays. This is for him.

—Arch Bell
(AusTexSoxFan)
Austin, TX

Win it for every Sox fan who has ever walked on this earth. Because they know how it feels to be used as a doormat by fans from other teams.

Win it for all those years of heartbreak.

Win it for all the naysayers.

Win it for loyalty.

Win it for peace of mind.

Win it for hope.

Win it for faith.

Win it because anything is possible.

Win it for all.

**—Jay Hreczuck
(Mendoza 13)
Blackstone, MA**

Win it for the 12-year-old kid who truly fell in love with the Sox in 1987. The kid that played solitaire while listening to every AM radio broadcast b/c the games were not on regular TV. The kid that loved Roger Clemens, Wade Boggs, Dwight Evans, Mike Greenwell, Jody Reed, Ellis Burks, Todd Benzinger, and a gang of other buzzards. The kid that hated the Yankees and their WPIX broadcasts in central NH—screw you, Phil Rizzuto. The kid that would rather watch baseball on Friday nights than go out with his friends. Nothing has changed.

Win it for my wife who has watched me flip out, break down, jump for joy, pray and fight for this team. How she has dealt with me—I don't know. Last year she finally became one of us.

Win it so my stepfather (a Yankee fan) can kiss my ass. So the words choke, curse, 1918 will not be the first thing he says to me every freakin' year.

Win it so Babe Ruth won't be portrayed as some mythical ghost sent to haunt Red Sox fans forever but as only one of the great ball players connected to the Sox.

—Matt McDaniel
(morassofnegativity)

Win it for my sister Patty.

Twenty-nine years ago a tragic car accident in college left 3 others dead and Patty in a coma for almost a year. Talk about courage, this lady has it in globs.

Mom and Dad were told to pull the plug, but they refused.

Patty came out of the coma, her mind intact, but body and voice broken.

Mom, Dad, and Patty follow the Red Sox everywhere.

Patty was just diagnosed with cancer 2 days ago.

Win it for Patty.

PS: Patty underwent successful cancer surgery in December and is expected to fully recover.

—Michael B. Hogan
Cranston, RI

Win it for Theodore Samuel Williams, who spent 5 of his best years in a Marine Corps rather than a Red Sox uniform.

Win it for my mom who died in 1991 much too early. A Bronx native, she surrendered whatever allegiance she had to NY teams when she married my dad and joined RSN.

Finally, and most important to me, win it for my old man. He's 75, kicking and a Fall River native who passed on his love for the Sox to me. Of course, we shared '75, '78, '86 and '03 together. I was only 1, though, in '67 (same age as my second son is now) and while I know he would have been thrilled to have shared the '67 Series with his only son, he instead was doing something more important—his duty in Vietnam. Now that he can finally enjoy a Series against the Cardinals, win it for him.

—Frank T. Pimentel

Win it for my dad, Joseph McGlone, who died suddenly in May at 52. I spent last year's playoffs on the phone with my father, calling after almost every play, wondering whether Oakland would be able to pull it together, rejoicing when they couldn't, and dissecting our chances against the Yankees. He was the last person I talked to after Boone's home run for almost a day straight, when I called crying, and was told, "There's always next year, Meg. Don't forget next year."

I fell in love with the Sox because of my dad, as something a 17-year-old girl could use as a communication device with a father entirely too much like her. He taught me the rules, and the history, and above all else, that no matter what they do to you, there is always a next year. Unfortunately, he wasn't so lucky. No more next years for him, but I'd like to think that he's part of the grand contingent of Red Sox Nation up there wheedling God to let us have one.

Win it for my good friend's grandfather who was just dignosed with terminal cancer and not given much longer to live. Big Sox fan. Please win one for him.

And win it for my grandmother, now 103 and in a nursing home. She's no longer as aware of things, but I remember all the afternoons on the couch with her, watching the Sox and the Pats (She really liked the tight pants on the players :)). Win one for those memories.

Win it for my dad who took me to my first Red Sox game and cemented me as a fan of this team for life. And who can't quite believe what's happening this October.

Win this for every Red Sox fan who's died a small death as the leaves changed.

Just win it.

—hoothehoo

Win it for all the Red Sox players I've had the honor of seeing their great play growing up and never got to win a championship with the Sox…. Yaz, Dewey, Jim Ed, Boggs, Eck, El Tiante, Bill Lee, Pudge, and even Roger…. we need to keep it going and polish off these MFY bastards and then take it all the way.

Also win it for my dad, Jack, a diehard Red Sox fan with whom I attended World Series Game 3 in 1986 with and sadly never lived long enough to see the great organization that the Red Sox have become today. He would be proud.

Win this game. Now.

—Doug Wedge
(Dennis Upperdeckersley)

Win it for ….

My grandfather, Mickey, was born in 1925 and grew up fast, big, and strong. His mother died of cancer at a young age and he went to work shortly thereafter to help support his younger brothers and sisters. Around that time, and I wish I knew how or where, he caught the eye of a baseball scout or two. New York Yankee scouts. For whatever reasons, most likely the dual mitigation of proximate family and a country at war, he turned them down cold.

Couldn't play for the Yankees. Only wanted to play for the Red Sox. Teddy Ballgame was his man.

And I'm not proud to say I listened with a raised eyebrow. By the time I was of age, he had gotten thick in the middle and balded in such fashion as to resemble a Sicilian Oliver Hardy. It was hard for me to get my twelve- or thirteen-year-old head around the notion that once upon a time, Grandpa had been a guy who could have played Major League Baseball.

Until one summer evening on the Cape. My dad and I were going down to a nearby school to shag flies after dinner, and Grandpa asked if he could come along. Or maybe he said he would come along, I don't remember. Now this was my mom's dad, so there was a bit of an interesting dynamic at play there—my dad and the older man he'd supplanted in many ways.

We got to the field and threw the ball around for a while, my dad hit some and Grandpa watched for a bit, then either asked if he could hit a few or was given the bat and encouraged to do so. Was I worried he'd embarrass himself? Maybe some, yeah. He was probably 58 or 59 at the time and I figured him for medium range on this little league field—if he got hold of one or two, that is. Still, I played him on the track.

But king hell speed if he didn't take that bat and hit the ball about a hundred feet over my head. I'm talking barrel of the bat, thirty feet high and rising on the Monster. And then he did it again. And again. Tossed the ball into the air, left hand sped back onto the bathandle and two hands through the hitting zone into a high finish. It was the most beautiful thing I'd seen in my life up to that point. I don't remember where my dad was playing; right then and there, it was my Grandpa and me.

The same way it was when he sat next to me on our couch when the Sox came back to beat the Angels in Game 5 of the 1986 ALCS. Before Henderson came to the plate, I was beside myself with fear, sadness, nervousness, and some kind of feeling I couldn't quite get at but would later remember as hope. He was, as ever in repose, impassive. Solid.

And after it had all happened…. "They did it," he said to me. "They're going to do it." He passed away the next November at the age of 62 and I miss him all the time, especially times like where we're sitting right now, on the precipice of history.

Win it for him, boys. For Mickey Collentro, my grandfather.

Mickey Collentro, a born cleanup hitter.

—Justin Keane

Win it for ....

Don't know if it's been said, but:

Win it for all of us who still don't believe in curses. If the unthinkable were to occur at this point, the minions of

Dan Shaughnessy would grow ad infinitum. This must not happen.

—Bucknahs Bum Ankle

Win it for my grandmother, Dottie who lives in Worcester, and has been rooting for the Sox for 70+ years. Her husband is sick and so she cannot attend many games, but has never missed a game on TV or the radio.

**—Ben Rubin
(IU Sox Fan5)
Swampscott, MA**

Win it for ....

My children, who have become as crazy about this team as I have been since I was 8. They have kept the faith better than I, because they weren't around to witness '75, '78, or '86. They have spent their childhood vacations watching the Sox wherever I forced them to, and finally got to see them in Fenway this year (thanks to a wonderful Sox fan, Angela Parker and Lenny Dinardo). They need to know that good things can happen in this world.

My father, although he isn't nearly the baseball fanatic that I am, he grew up outside of Boston and took me to my first game in Fenway back in '76. Although he and I don't talk to each other very often, he did attend the game with my family at Fenway this year. It is because of his childhood home that I am the Sox fan that I am. I've never lived in Boston, but my heart has always been there.

My wife, because she married me 15 years ago not knowing what she was getting into, and she still loves me and now loves the Sox almost as much as I do. She has taken to reading the game threads on SoSH and reading the better posts to me as I squirm on the couch watching these games.

Last of all, win it for my buddy, Jim Lapworth (1954-2004), a lifelong New York Yankees fan that I know would have been in my face after game 3 and would have been hiding from me after game 7. He died earlier this year after a long battle with cancer and I miss having him around to talk baseball to. Even though he was a MFY fan, I know he would be pulling for the Sox with me now.

**—Mike Moore
(Rhavisi)**

Win it for my grandad Naldo who was born in 1899 and died in 1972 and my father Gerald (favorite player Ted Williams) who was born in 1923 and died in 1994 who both were potato farmers in Aroostook County, Maine. Win it for my brothers Len (favorite player Jimmy Piersall) and Clint (favorite player Jackie Jenson), both great teachers in Maine. Our family had the outfield covered. Win it for me, who always drafted the Red Sox players in my APBA leagues and have followed them from Hawaii for the last 35 years. Win it for my daughter Megan, a huge David Ortiz fan attending the

University of Oregon. Win it for all the long suffering fans. Win it today!

—Reg Worthley
Hawaii

Win it for my grandfather who passed away at the young age of 74 on April 1, 2004. He faithfully followed the Red Sox year in and year out and I know he's up there with Ted Williams fighting off the age-old demons so the Red Sox can reach the pinnacle.

—Evan Brunell

Win it for an old man who took his grandson to every bar on the way to Fenway, feeding the boy a cheeseburger and sucking down a beer himself at each stop, greeting everyone by name, and getting utterly perplexed when the boy was too full for a Fenway frank once they took their seats somewhere between the first base line and the Pesky Pole.

Win it for that little boy who felt like a king every time his grampy hoisted him onto the bar stool. Win it for him because his father was a Yankee fan, and he listened to his grampy instead.

Win it for that little boy, who is now a grown man and the best father a kid, young or old, could ask for. His life hasn't gone as planned. He has given up so much for his family. And the only time he has missed one of his son's baseball games was when he was in the hospital. Win it for him for passing on his love of baseball to his children and letting them learn life lessons through the Boston Red Sox.

Win it for the little boy's little boy, who is not so little anymore. He is the future, and he throws a knuckleball too. Win it for him because he practices the standards of the Shade Foundation on the baseball field after precancerous moles were removed from him when he was twelve. Win it for him, and all the little kids like him, who were sent to bed early last year and woke up thinking that the Red Sox were going to the World Series. Win it for all the parents who had to explain otherwise.

Win it for the woman who was used to watching Braves games all season, but gave that up for the satellite package that allowed us to watch the Red Sox all summer. Win it for her for putting up with the yelling, the crying, the throwing things, and being told, "You already know what it's like to see your team win it all!"

My brother, my father, my mother, and the great-grandfather I never knew. Win it for them.

—Amy Rossi

Win it for my father Merle, who took me to my first few games at Fenway Park, starting in August 1976. He wasn't a huge baseball fan, but I did find out years after death in 1982 that Jimmy Piersall appeared in several commercials for his father's country store in northern Vermont.

Win it for my mom Peggy, who I taught to score games. We had our bad times/years, but I appreciated her scoring the 1978 playoff game as I pedaled home from high school like Lance Armstrong.

Win it for my oldest friend Ray, still loyal to the Red Sox and living up in Essex Junction, Vermont. Friends since high school, we watched a lot of the 1986 playoffs together. We had the corks ready to pop on 63 George Street in Burlington late on that October night, but it wasn't to be. A few hours after Game 7 ended, we drank them anyway and he fell asleep on my bathroom floor, hugging a huge wrench. .... I hope he can come down to Boston for the eventual parade.

Win it for all the nuts who love this team more than is probably healthy. A lot of those people hang out here and I can barely express how happy I have been for the knowledge and laughs I've gotten over the past few years.

Win it for all of those older-than-old ladies we see on NESN each night, who say they have watched "every Sox game since 1653." No other team has such dedicated fans.

Win it for, as Big Papi says, "Boston Nation".

—Allan Wood

Win it for Grandpa Lee, who wrote lovingly of the Sox in his diary on the troop ship going over to France in 1918, and who took me to my first game at Fenway in Teddy Ballgame's last season. Win it for Dad, who's waited 81 years and will never give up. And win it for Jonathan and Andrew, because my happiest memories in the last five years have been sitting with them in Fenway during our annual July pilgrimmage.

—Jeff Lee

Win it for my father, who had a love for numbers, and baseball, and passed it on to me, it was the only way we could communicate, but was always a safe haven and at least there was ONE way to communicate, he died last year, and his birthday, was October 20th, the day the Red Sox beat the Yankees!

Win it for my mother, who died when I was 9, on October 2nd, 1967, the day the Red Sox won the pennant, and the day I became both a Red Sox fan, and also a single parented child.

And PLEASE win it for every single person I know or have ever met, who I'm sure have suffered with my insane passion for the Red Sox, and most have no idea why I am like this, and many even say it is just a game (haha imagine that!) please win it for them, so they don't have to always hear me going on about the Sox (as if I'll stop after we win it all)!

—Cheekydave

Win it for ....

I'm writing this from Ireland, where I live now with my wife and two small boys. Win this for them. It's a bit hard to give them a sense of where their father is from—America sometimes is just an abstract notion of a place that appears on the news or in the movies or on a vacation. The Red Sox and the sense of community they bring are the best advertisement the country ever had. Win it for them so that they can associate happy endings with the Red Sox, this most solid, valid and enjoyable of institutions.

I was at the game previously mentioned on this thread where Jim Rice went into the crowd to help the kid who got hit by a line foul. I was there when Mike Greenwell got an inside the park grand slam against the MFY. At my bachelor party in August of '97 Mo hit a three run walkoff homer to win. I've been at three division clinching games and countless other great times at Fenway. The Sox were never cursed—they've always been blessed with the best place to play, the best fans and the best history. Its just that there is something missing—one gap to be filled in. Close the circle—win it for all of us.

—Michael Shea

Win it for Neildo (my dad!) so my father, who grew up in a Yankee family and chose the Red Sox instead, doesn't have to take crap from the rest of the family during the holidays.

WIN IT for my pop, who has given his two daughters his passion, obsession and love for the Red Sox. There is nothing better than a game, a beer, and my dad.

WIN IT for my dad who, after the Red Sox went down 0-3 vs. the Yankees, called me and said, "We've got them right where we want 'em." That's BELIEVING. And as usual, he was right.

WIN IT for my mom for putting up with the whole bunch of us, and leaving me voicemails with score updates when I can't watch.

Finally, WIN IT for Wil D.: a dear friend who passed on when we were 17, who loved the Red Sox more than anyone and is watching this with a big smile on his face. This one's for you, buddy.

—Pam Lombardi
(SoxChick13)
Proud Member of Red Sox Nation living in NYC
Proud Daughter of Neil Lombardi

Win it for my uncle, Luke Davis. He was born in West Texas at the turn of the century and migrated to California in the early 1920s. He worked in the oilfields until an accident there left him unable to work.

He did public spirited things like serving on the Water Commission in Orange County (no small thing in an arid environment converted to agriculture and then a major population base).

But his passion was teaching kids to play ball. Not merely play ball, but play it the right way, the old school way. He coached the Little League ball for close to forty years. For the last twenty or so he had an unusual way of picking his players. He'd tell the other coaches, "You go ahead and pick the kids you want. When you're done, I'll take the rest." He got the uncoordinated and the hard cases—and yes, there are nine-year-old hard cases. Somehow those kids won the league championship more often than not.

The Bad News Bears? Not hardly. If you played for Luke, you had short hair. Your ballcap never left your head. Your shirttail was tucked in. You played hard, but you played clean. And, by God, you could (and would) lay down a bunt if you were given the signal. Even taking the scrubs, he had a couple of kids who later made it to the big leagues. He was proud of them, but no prouder than he was of other kids who grew up to be doctors or mechanics, kids who grew up to be good fathers and who would then do anything that they could to get their kids on Luke's team.

When he went into his nineties, things got Mister Chips like. They had a major banquet/birthday party in his honor so that he could hear the kids he coached tell what he meant to their lives. They also named the ballfield in Costa Mesa "Luke Davis Field." I lived 3000 or so miles away and missed that night, to my regret.

He wasn't a saint. Many of his attitudes reflected his early days. But a boy was a boy and a ballplayer was a ballplayer, and that's what mattered. He was a special worshipper (and minister) in the Great Church of Baseball.

I said to win this for him. That might not be entirely appropriate since every one of those Little League teams was named the Cardinals. So don't win it for him, but honor what he was by winning it well.

—Bill Manson

Win it for Helen Robinson, who'll be fielding every congratulatory phone call on heaven's switchboard.

Win it for Joe Foy, Jerry Adair, Bob Tillman, Don McMahon, Ken Brett, John Wyatt, and Elston Howard whose efforts 37 autumns ago nearly brought us the Impossible Dream.

Win it for the Johnsons—Darrell and Deron, the only departed members of the '75 Sox.

Win it for Tom and Jean Yawkey. Say what you want about how they ran the team—all they ever wanted to do was win.

Win it for Ray Fitzgerald, Jerry Nason, and Ernie Roberts—three ex-*Globe* scribes who wrote about the Sox with class, dignity, and style.

Win it for Nuf Ced McGreevy and all the original Royal Rooters.

Win it for Bill Buckner, so his name is finally erased from the blackboard of blame.

Win it for Lawrence Adrian Brown, who passed in 2000 at age 94. Sure, they won it while he was alive, the last time when he was 12, but it rings hollow when you don't hear about it for a week—and then only via word of mouth because you grew up poor in rural Maine. Enjoy this one, Gramp.

—Mark Brown

Win it for my childhood idols, Jim Rice and Dewey Evans.

Win it for the great friends I have made over the years all because of a single bond—our love of baseball.

Win it to finally take away the pain of my first sleepless experience over a sporting event (Oct. '86—12 years old at the time).

Win it for the diehards on this board and all across RSN who have patiently waited their entire lifetimes for the pinnacle achievement in all of sports.

Win it for my girlfriend (now my fiancée), who has put our lives on hold over the past few weeks so her boyfriend could live out his dream. Thank you, Kim.

Win it for my mom who told me stories about the "great" Duke Snider she used to idolize growing up.

Mom, thanks for sharing your love of baseball with me and passing along your passion.

And finally, win it for my dad, who accompanied me to the game that started this marvelous run—Game 4 ALCS. Dad, you will always be my favorite "good luck charm."

ONE MORE WIN!!!

**—Jamie Ross
(Rossox)**

Win it for JWH, LL, and Tom Werner who are exactly what this team needed. They have done something that the previous ownership groups haven't; they gave back to the fans that give so much for this organization. I thank you three and hope you have the joy of presenting Boston with its first World Series win in 86 years.

Folks, we aren't just fans, we aren't just a nation, hell we aren't even a brotherhood; we are something more important than that, we are a family.

From April to October we have watched the games together. Take a quick look at the game threads. We could all watch the games at home and stay off of our beloved SoSH but we continue to post while watching the game. The reason for this is that we are all friends and enjoy each other's company while watching our favorite team. Throughout the struggles of this season, we all stuck together and watched in awe as our 25 heroes rallied for another breathtaking win.

Take a look back, April to October is a long time. From the cold rainy days of April to the dog days of summer to the crisp nights of early fall, we have been supporting this team. Opening Day we drove through neighborhoods of budding trees and bright flowers to get to Fenway. In the summer we squinted our eyes as a picturesque sun set against the backdrop of the press boxes. The red and oranges of the sun clashed with the green of the grass to form dramatic painting right before our eyes. Once September arrived, the lights were turned on earlier in the game. The wind had a slight chill to it that reminded us of all that was good. When I imagine heaven, I imagine myself sitting in box seats on a warm summer night with my best friends.

Win or lose this season has been extraordinary.

I just want to thank all of you. Your vast baseball knowledge has kept me up to 3:00 a.m. on many school/work nights.

**—Nick DiMaio
(mrcleanwell)**

Win it for ....

My grandparents (and my family)....

My grandparents: They are in their 80s and there was nothing I wanted more than to have a Red Sox World

Series win for them in their lifetime. As I was growing up, I can't recall all the times I've been to their house or they've been to mine and we've huddled around the radio or TV to watch/hear a game. I've since moved away and those times are few and far between, if they exist at all, but I will hold onto those memories forever.

I spoke to my grandmother yesterday and tried to explain that I've been waiting for a Series win. How I've lived through the pain for 20+ years (I'm 28), not thinking that I'm talking to a woman who not only knows what I'm talking about, but has been through so much more for so much longer. My grandmother lives in Barre, MA, (just outside Worcester) with my grandfather and she can talk shop with the best of them.... about the Sox, the Huskies, the Patriots, education, government.... you name it. Just try her. My grandfather knows his stuff too.... I just would never argue with him. I love her and my grandfather.... they are typical Sox fans, and through thick and through thin they've seen it all and have been to the brink of ultimate frustration and now the ultimate.... A Sox World Series Victory! I love them and am glad they are with us to experience this!!!

And to my family: To my mother, father, and my sister. My mother who has grown up with this as the daughter of my grandparents. A New Englander virtually all her life, she isn't the biggest of fans, but she honestly never ceases to amaze me. And my father who grew up in Ohio and has been brainwashed (effectively I might add) to become a diehard fan (even though I had to wake him with a phone call the minute they won the Series).

Before, I used to say fortunately he didn't have to grow up with the "disease" of being a Sox fan. He could never understand how I seemingly would die on the inside when the Sox would lose. He told me that there were much worse things going on in life than the Sox losing to the Yanks in '03…. I knew this, but it didn't make the hurt go away. But now, I wish he did grow up with it like I did, because what I feel is beyond anything describable…. the hurt is replaced with sheer joy.

Truth is though, my first passion lies within the sport of baseball and it was my father who taught me how to play the game, and my mom who encouraged every moment! To play the game and to be a Red Sox fan is the ultimate and I'm glad I can still do/be both. And to my sister who called me several times the week of the Series, but I wouldn't call back until I knew it was in the bag. When it was said and done, she knew I was ignoring her, but she called me anyway…. I won't ever forget the time she volunteered to play on my baseball team in little league and got beaned, I almost started a bench-clearing brawl just to stick up for her…. but the fact that she got up there with the big boys was enough to show me that baseball was always going to have a place in my life and in my family's life.

I love them all and wish I could've shared this with them.

To my wife: A couple weeks ago, I got married and shared this with my newest love, Whitney. A wedding followed by a honeymoon in Mexico is not the easiest thing to experience during the playoffs. It all seemed over on our 2nd to last night in paradise, so I had to pretend I didn't care. Our last night I didn't even get a chance to watch the game. I convinced myself that I didn't want to so if they lost my depression wouldn't waste away our last memories of our trip. Waking up the next morning to see the headlines, Sox Win, was a tease, so I told myself not to buy into it as much (they were still down 1-3). The plane ride home was one of the most heart wrenching as the pilot kept announcing the score as the Yanks and Sox battled to a 4-4 tie.... until we arrived in Atlanta and I heard a Sox fan yell they won. The rest is history as they won games 6, 7 and the Series.

Wow!

My wife and I have celebrated two UCONN Huskies NCAA championships, two Patriots Super Bowls and now this.... a Red Sox World Series (too surreal to even write down). Lets hope I can add the number 2 next to the Sox to balance out this list. As for my wife, I love her, not for the fact they won of course, but for standing by me even when I haven't been the most fun person to be with during the ups and the downs.

Thanks for giving me a forum, guys.... I love you all!!!

—Seth Dieter

Win it for ....

I'd like the Sox to win it for my father-in-law who passed away a few years ago. He was a lifelong Sox fan who grew up in Greenfield, MA, and when he lived on the Cape would take his youngest daughter, who is now my wife, to Fenway whenever he could. Besides his family and golf the Red Sox were the biggest passion in his life. His name was Joe Boissy. He was a good man.

He never got to see what I took my children to see.

**—Rick Rowand
(absintheofmalaise)**

Win it for Patty Sakalaukus, from Lakeville, Mass., a good friend of ours and a huge Sox fan, killed earlier this spring in a bizarre rollover accident. She loved the Sox—especially Jason Varitek, and hopefully she'll have front row seats for the Championship when it finally becomes a reality!

—kevlog

Win it for ....

I've lurked for about a year now and its been such a thrill to see my own thoughts, fears, happy moments and everything else reflected in the posts I see on this board. Baseball IS sentiment, but what you've created here goes beyond what even I could hope for. It is the best in all of us. So, if I may, I'd be so honored if you could post my contribution.

For my cousin who drives up to Boston from behind enemy lines for games. He can't make it to every single game, but people like him who have seasons tickets—and generously shared them—are what makes this so special. His generosity has given me some very special memories.

For my uncle and my Dad, who have waited a long time for this, but never wavered. And taught me many things about the game along the way.

For my brothers, who are all going to be watching tonight. And just like any other game night, I'll know when they're going to call before the phone even rings.

For my Mom who never much understood the ins and outs of baseball, but was happy to turn in her old Mass. license plates before this season and exchange them for the Red Sox Jimmy Fund plates, in the hopes that this would help.

Lastly, for my late grandfather. As I think back, Red Sox games looked sweeter on his old cranky TV than they do now on mine. I know he is part of this, so thank you Papa!

—Kitty Baseball

Win it for Paul McNeil (1916-1983). Win it for his wife, Lynn, who is still alive and kicking at 82 years young.

Win it for their son, Andrew, my father.

Win it for my son, Kyle, born a mere 5 months ago and new to this roller-coaster ride.

Win it for yourselves. Win it for Boston. Win it for all of us. Win it so that no one can ever say that it was foolish to have hope. Because without hope, we are nothing.

—The Allented Mr Ripley

Win it for yourselves and for all of Red Sox Nation both here and departed.

Make yourselves legends in this city.

Win it for my dad, who never was allowed to play the game other than on sandlots or on military bases while stationed overseas because of his strict dad. He gave me the bug, and was always there growing up to watch a game with or to teach me the game, to coach my teams, to work with me on the side, even when I was too stubborn to listen. Win it for my dad so I can celebrate with him. He never lost faith in this team.

**—Mike Sweeney
(NickEsasky)**

Win it for ....

For my grandfather who threw a no-hitter in high school, but went off to WWII and earned a Purple Heart before he could think about pursuing a baseball career.

Pop almost single-handedly indoctrinated me with my Sox-love and Yankee-hate. One of my earliest memories was a trip to Fenway with him and my father, when they made me recite the chant, "Yay Red Sox! Boo Yankees!" over and over. He and my father taught me to pitch and to love the game. They taught me how to carry myself on the field, and how to handle adversity. They watched me strike out 17 in a 6-inning game when I was 12. They watched me score the winning run in a key game of my Little League tournament. They taught me how to be successful but also how to handle a loss. And they taught me to love the Red Sox.

Pop used to be friends with an usher named Fitz, I believe, who upon receipt of a fin ($5) would escort my grandfather and whomever he was with to whatever the best seats near the dugout were. There, he'd sit and yell at Yaz whenever he got a big hit, "I love you, you big dumb beautiful [insert Polish slur here]!" And yes, Yaz would look over in askance as he could hear Pop quite clearly.

In the '75 World Series, he, my father, mother, and sister (in utero) went to Fenway without tickets and sat on the steps between sections in a sold-out Fenway thanks to good ol' Fitz.

Pop got to see '46, '67, '75, and '86, but he never got to see the Red Sox win a World Series. He saw the entire careers of Lefty Grove, Jimmy Foxx, Joe Cronin, Bobby Doerr, Ted Williams, Carl Yastrzemski, Carlton Fisk, and Dwight Evans.

He got to see Roger Clemens just until his career with the Sox ended. And he got to see Nomar as a September call-up in '96, and pronounced he would become a really special player. It was in the spring of '97 that we spread Pop's ashes from the front row on the first base side in Fenway, before Nomar hit 30 home runs in his first full year, before Pedro no-hit the Indians over 6 in the playoffs, before the end of the Duquette/Harrington era, before the start of a sabermetrically aware and fiscally responsible management, before the end of the Yankees' WS run, before the Sox started to challenge the notion of a Yankees' dynasty by coming 5 outs away from beating them to the World Series, before Curt Schilling earned his Red Sox by bleeding into his sock in the most gut-wrenching, gritty, and courageous pitching performance he would have ever seen, and before THIS team made history by toppling the Yankees' World Series hopes in their own ballpark after being down 0-3 in the most important Red Sox triumph I have ever seen.

My grandfather Red, Bud, Bill, or Pop would be damn proud of this year's team. They've won 105 games since April, and I think he'd say it's the best Sox team he'd ever seen. I know he'd believe. I believe. They just need four more wins. Go Sox!

—Aaron Herdman
(Arock78)

Win it for ....

I'd like to add my father to the list as well. He has been a steady and loyal Sox fan for nearly 60 years through many difficult personal battles, not the least of which was the passing of my sister in 1983. For his 50th birthday (a few years later), my mother and I sent him to the Red Sox Fantasy Camp in Florida. He spent hours with Bobby Doerr, Luis Tiant, Bernie Carbo, Dick Radatz, and many others. He talks to this day about roping a double off El Tiante and paying the price of hours in the trainer's room as a result (pulled muscles he didn't know he had). No matter how down he may be at anytime (and he's never been the same since her death), I'm always able to cheer him up by asking about the night he spent at the bar with Teddy Ballgame. He bought the Splinter a few Old Grandads and was honored with a conversation that included the art of hitting as well as a few lectures on other topics. Ted wouldn't sign a ball for him, but said he would for my mom. Dad always spoke so highly of him that I regret never having had the opportunity to meet him myself. Dad gave me the ball a few years back with the warning that I had better never sell it. I wouldn't care if someone offered me a thousand dollars, it's worth so much more to me because of how much it means to him.

I grew up a Yaz fan and when Dad's co-workers presented him with an autographed Yaz bat at his retirement, he immediately gave it to me. My favorite memory as a kid comes from the day that he and I (along with my uncle and cousin) took the train into Boston for a day at

Fenway. Dad got us seats in the left field corner so that I could see Yaz up close and personal. I'll also never forget the night he sat outside Fenway park after sitting through a rainy doubleheader of losses while I waited for Yaz to walk out to his car. My sister had passed away recently and I'm sure that sitting in the car in the rain after those two tough losses so that I could get Yaz's autograph was pretty low on his list of things to do, but he did it for me and our love of the Sox.

That's how it is with the two of us. I'm still trying to get World Series tickets and I don't care if I have to drive to Missouri or Massachusetts, I'm determined to give him the gift of seeing them live in the WS. The Red Sox have become more than a bond between us; they transcend so many things.

As much as I want to see a World Championship, it just won't be the same if it doesn't happen in my dad's lifetime. I'm certain that there are many of you out there that know exactly what I mean.

Also, I'd like the Sox to win it for my kids so that they never have to hear Dan Shaughnessy's nonsense about a "curse." I'd like them to grow up optimists, unlike their old man who has witnessed 1967, 1975, 1978, 1986, and so much more along with all of you.

—Michael Huntoon
(Yaz4Ever)

Win it for ....

I am a first-generation native New Englander. My parents grew up in Queens, NY, but thankfully were Dodger fans and Yankee-Haters. They moved to Boston in 1965, arriving with me in utero on the night of the Great Northeast Blackout.

Unlike so many of you, I was not fortunate enough to inherit my love for the Sox from father or grandfather. But Lynn, Yaz, Fisk, Scott, Tiant and Lee got me hooked at age nine, and I've never looked back.

In fact, my passion for the team has swum upstream a generation, and my parents are now fans. Dad called me with two outs in the 9th inning of Game 7 last week, and for a second I felt like we were a couple of ten-year-olds, giggling at our good fortune. After he hung up, I thought of how it must have been for him as a teenager in 1955, when his beloved Brooklyn Bums finally overcame their own Yankees jinx.

I live in the heart of enemy territory now. I miss my adoptive homeland and its extended Red Sox Nation family, especially at this time of year, when the leaves are changing and we're so used to moth-balling our dreams for another winter.

I'll never forget how New England came together in the fall of '86, when I was on the verge of shaking hands with every stranger on the street and hugging my sour-pussed convenience store cashier. I'll never forget how awful it felt to have that sense of unity and shared pride ripped from us at the last moment, or how many times since then that I've wondered if it would ever come back.

Win it for me, Red Sox, so I can have that feeling again.

**—Russell Kellogg
(RusterK)**

Win it for my grandpa, George, whom I remember best sitting in front of the TV yelling at his Red Sox, and who died in 1991, a decade plus too early.

Win it for my dad, Paul, who bought me my first glove and Red Sox cap by age 4. Every year was "the year" for us…. and always will be, still. I hope to sip some Jameson's with him as we cry and laugh and hug, and toast my grandpa later this week. My dad is my real hero, and I am glad he passed on his Sox lunacy to me. I LOVE every heart wrenching, stomach turning, yelling and crying and cheering and believing second of it.

And lastly, win it for the 12-year-old girl who ran around the made-up bases in her backyard in '86 after Hendu bailed us out, and who cried the real tears of a broken heart later that month. I left her somewhere in that backyard 18 years ago, and I'd like to bring her home, at last.

Thanks to all you guys and gals on SoSH…. I didn't think being a Sox fan needed to get better, but when I started my daily (ok, hourly) lurking, I realized how much better it can be. You are all wonderful!

**—April Fitzpatrick
(DESOXFAN)**

Win it for Grandma and Grandpa Starrett. They taught my mother and I how to truly love baseball.

Win it for Grandma Anderson who told me just before she passed that she was pretty sure they would win one sometime soon.

Win it for Grandpa Anderson with the Hope that this may briefly pierce the shroud of Alzheimer's that surrounds this noble man.

Win it for Mom and me; we have agreed to only speak briefly after each game mostly to see if we are both still alive.

Win it for my wife Rebecca who suffers all my Red Sox angst with grace.

Win it for my daughter who is watching the games at UCSD. She reminds me of a lonely freshmen at RPI in 1978. May she met some lifelong friends like I did so long ago.

Win it for us all.

**—Richard Anderson
(Harry Agganis)**

Win it for every child (or child at heart) who has had their heart broken in the past, but kept coming back each year.

Win it for my 73-year-old dad. His faith in the team has often been bent, but has never broken. After Game 5, he told me, "I'm so damn proud to be a Red Sox fan."

Win it for my 90-plus-year-old Aunt Stella. She can't see or hear too well, but she never misses a game.

Win it for the Nation.

—Mike Medeiros

Win it for ....

OK, close to sobbing now....

Win it for longtime Sox PR and Community Affairs exec Dick Bresciani, the epitome of class and dignity, who has fielded my calls with aplomb for nearly 20 years.

Win it for the fans in Yankee territory (including my own two kids and this 47-year-old kid) who are taunted each year by arrogant Yankee fans.

**—Greg Brodsky
(NJ Fan)**

Win it for all the members of Red Sox Nation who never stopped believing.

Win it for all the great players who have played for this franchise and never won it all.

Win it for Teddy %@*&# Ballgame, the greatest hitter who ever lived.

Win it for the heroes of my youth who showed me that baseball is the best game of all: Rice, Lynn, Fisk, Remy, Eck, Dewey, Boggs and all the others.

Win it especially for Yaz, who deserved it so much and said goodbye with class and grace.

Win it for the 1986 Red Sox who gave me one of the best summers of my life and took us to the brink. Win it for Hendu, who almost got us there. Win it for Bill Buckner, who always gave it his all and earned a better legacy than he got.

Win it for Ned Martin, who thrilled me on a lazy summer afternoon when after a meaningless Tony Armas home run, he called out my name on the air and said that I was "another winner in the TV38 Home Run Sweepstakes." Mercy.

Win it for all the guys I watched the '86 Series with at Paul C's house in Old Saybrook and regret that I have lost touch with over the years.

Win it for my buddy Jamie, who flew in from India just to be in Boston when it happens.

Win it for my great uncle Henry Reilly who died in 2000 at the age of 93, barely remembering the last Red Sox title and hoping he would live to see another one.

Win it for my sister Kara and her children, Dylan and Katie, who, like the Sox, have fought back from adversity this year and will come out on top.

Win it for my mother, who beat cancer in the summer of Morgan Magic, who is beating it again during this magical run, and who fell in love with this year's team.

Win it for my father, who took me to my first game at Fenway, who took me to Yaz Day, who took me to the last game of the '81 Series so I could see the MFY lose in person, and who will be with me in the stands if there is a Game 7. Thanks, Dad.

Finally, win it for my wife, who has put up with a lot of mood swings depending on the team's fortunes, who has stayed with me in the bleachers on cold and rainy nights in April, who is beginning to understand why this means so much, and who always finds a way to make me smile. Thank you for everything Bee.

—John Chayrigues

Win it for my daughter, who while never having lived in New England, is a Red Sox fan because of her obsessive/compulsive mother.

I tried to talk her out being a Sox fan after last year's devastation, but she told me now she understood the pain I felt.

As we sat holding hands and watching the final outs in this years game 7, I thanked God that her twelve-year-old heart would not feel the years of pain I have felt since Bucky Dent broke my twelve-year-old heart.

—Kate Handley
(bosoxgrl)

Win it for ....

The Boston Red Sox are 27 outs away from winning the World Series.

Twenty-seven outs away from something my grandfather never got to see.

Twenty-seven outs away from being able to share that experience with my dad.

Twenty-seven outs that one of my best friends Shawn never got to see, as he was on United 175 that hit the Tower Two on 9/11. He was a Yankee fan and would've enjoyed the whole postseason.

Twenty-seven outs away from retiring the "19-18" chant.

Twenty-seven outs away from having eight and eighty-year olds dance for joy. And cry for the same reason.

Twenty-seven outs away from Babe Ruth being just another dead Yankee.

Twenty-seven outs away from Ted Williams smiling in heaven. And swearing at Joe DiMaggio.

Twenty-seven outs away from Johnny Pesky holding a trophy, and not the ball.

Twenty-seven outs away from Dom DiMaggio smiling and dialing Bobby Doerr's phone number.

Twenty-seven outs away from Derek Lowe mirroring Joe Dobson's career-best game five performance in 1946 versus St. Louis.

Twenty-seven outs away from the new Impossible Dream.

Twenty-seven outs away from vindication for Tony C, Rico, Yaz, and Gentleman Jim Lonborg.

Twenty-seven outs away from glory.

Twenty-seven outs away from becoming the New Big Red Idiot Machine.

Twenty-seven outs away from Carbo and Fisk's home runs not going for naught.

Twenty-seven outs away from one for Luis, Dewey, Freddie, the Rooster, and the Spaceman.

Twenty-seven outs away from Bucky Dent going back to being just another crummy .247 career hitting shortstop.

Twenty-seven outs away from forgetting the name Mike Torrez.

Twenty-seven outs away from being one strike away.

Twenty-seven outs away from forgetting the Steamer's wild pitch.

Twenty-seven outs away from restoring Bill Buckner's legacy as a career .289 hitter, with 2715 career hits and the 1980 Silver Slugger award.

Twenty-seven outs away from Dan Shaughnessy having to invent a new phrase.

Twenty-seven outs away from forgiving Wade Boggs and the horse he rode in on.

Twenty-seven outs away from hoping Grady gets another chance.

Twenty-seven outs away from Aaron Boone being a question mark at the hot corner for the Cleveland Indians in 2005.

Twenty-seven outs away from someday retiring No. 21 and forgiving Roger for the Blue Jays and the Yanks. Well, two out of three ain't bad.

Twenty-seven outs away from winning it all.

So Red Sox, do just that: win it for all.

**—Mike Laprey
(romine16)**

Win it for RSN, SoSH members everywhere and for Shaun who is the most poetic among us.

Win it for all my Weston buddies who put up with this baseball nut growing up and with whom I could always count on to see the Sox at Fenway. Win it for Eddie (Rico), Rick (Brooksie), Derby, Billy, Goodie, Mike, Chuck, Freddy and all the rest.

Win it for my first LL coach Tom Adams whose love for and knowledge of the game brought me great joy and made me a fan for life. He was the best coach I ever had. Win it for his sons especially "Acey."

Win it for all the kids who have gone to sleep with a Sox hat on their bedpost and a baseball glove on their hand.

Win it for all the people who earn their living working for this organization. They deserve it so much.

Win it for all of us who will always BELIEVE and who are bound by this common thread.

**—Matt Livingston
(SoxFanSince57)**

Win it for my Grandfather Edgar Kelley. For it was the Red Sox that allowed a 70-plus-year-old man and a young teenager to have countless meaningful conversations. The pure, unadulterated bashing of Wade Boggs provided a bond from one generation, to the next, to the next. And there was nothing wrong with Johnny Mac, he was a good Irishman. Although it may have been the Sox that killed him, he's giving me a big High Five after every win.

And win it for my father Dick Kelley. After game 7 last year he insisted this team was cursed, and that he was done pouring his heart into them. He was as frustrated as fan could be. Last week, we laughed at how silly of a statement that was, as we both knew he wouldn't be gone for long. May the Sox win so he doesn't have to go back on any more statements next year.

Win it for my stepdad Scott Robinson, who insists on calling me every 6 hours to discuss the Sox, literally. After the last three games he's called to complain about Pedro going in in the 7th or the 4 errors, instead of just being happy about the win. He's an emotional wreck. He insists that he doesn't get emotionally attached to big league ballplayers that get paid millions. We both know he's full of $hit and he's as excited as anyone about the

Sox being in the series. I know this because he lives out of state so the calls are a neccessity as he's fiending for good information, and he's almost come to fist to cuffs with two Yankees fans in the last week. Win it for him so he'll have nothing left to be nervous about.

And finally win it for my wife Kim. She's may be the biggest Sox fan this side of the Charles River. She's waited in line for 7 hours this fall to snag day of game tickets, she's made it through to the Sox ticket office for playoff tickets and she looks really hot in her Curt Schilling t-shirt. There's no one I'd rather debate a pinch hit move with during the game....

And don't forget me…. Because I want it bad.

**—Rick Kelley
(rskelley75)**

Win it for all of us who have walked through the entrance at Fenway the first time to see the radiant green on a brilliant Saturday afternoon. I have had the pleasure of providing the same to my son, Thomas, this past summer. It is an image that never fades.

Win it for Tom Kennedy, who was the grandfather I never had. Tom was a true fan. His words always sounded like poetry, especially when the subject was the Red Sox.

Win it for my dad who was with me in '67, '75, and '86. He always reminded me who was "due." Now we are all "due."

—Jim DiCiaccio
(Coopercats)

Win it for ....

I cried reading this thread and I wanted to add....

Win it for my father, "Dale" Earlywine who died in 2002 of cancer. He moved to Massachusetts while my mother was pregnant with me and has been a Red Sox fan since 1980. He would have been so proud to see them "spank the yanks" and then go all the way. My boyfriend Brian Meddows is also a diehard fan and he would be quite happy also. Win it for all of Red Sox Nation! WE BELIEVE....

—Marcia Earlywine
Marlborough, Massachusetts

Win it for ....

Okay, I am finally chiming in here:

Win it for each and every Red Sox player from 1919 on who played hard every day, finding ways to win, giving it their all, their hearts and souls, hoping each spring that this would be the year they would win the World Series.

Win it for the Cubs fans, the Giants fans, the Astros fans and all the other teams that have languished without a World Series win for decades. The ones that, when the Red Sox finally reign, will have a little more hope each spring that this can be the year, that maybe there really is no such thing as a curse, that anything can happen if you believe. Win it for those anguished, tortured, waiting fans—the ones the Red Sox Nation used to be.

Win it for all the new fans that will now begin to live and die with the Red Sox and all the fans that have lived and died with this team for 86 years.

—Mary-Colleen Tinney

Win it for....

My father was a Red Sox fan since 1954 and listened to the Impossible Dream on military radio when he was away for the Vietnam War. He loved three grown men in his life: his dad, Y.A. Tittle and Ted Williams. My father passed his love of the Red Sox along to me as if it were a gilded and precious family heirloom. He taught me how to swear at Don Zimmer and he cried as hard as I did after Game 6. Through the years the Red Sox were the one thing we had in common and my love of the Red Sox is so entwined in my love for my father that it's impossible to tell where one ends and the other begins.

My father was as excited as everyone on this site when Schilling agreed to come to the Red Sox. About a month later my dad was diagnosed with advanced pancreatic

carcinoma and he never even made it to the Grapefruit
League season, never mind the magic that was the 2004
Red Sox run. When Renteria tapped back weakly to
Foulke I swear I heard a gossamer whimper emanate
from the ephemeral and that somewhere my dad was
crying as hard as me and saying "finally I can rest in
Peace." So Rest in Peace Pop.

Oh, and I always suspected he was a jinx so he dies and
they win it. I KNEW it!!

—Jason Masters

Win it for my dad, James Devlin (1933-1989), and all of the other
departed Sox fans who gave their all for this team and
never were able to see their beloved Sox win it all.

Win it for us, whose love of all things Red Sox has
remained strong in the modern media era despite suffering the slings and arrows of outrageous fools who peddle
the myths of nonexistent ghosts and curses.

Win it for my 12-year-old son Ryan and all of the
younger members of the Nation, because some childhood dreams should end in a victory parade.

I will always identify the 2003-04 Red Sox with my son.
I had attempted when he was young to share my love of
baseball and the Red Sox with him, but those early
efforts were met with only lukewarm enthusiasm on his
part. In recent years, though, he gradually became an
avid fan of the game, and he proudly adopted the Sox as

his team because he was a native Bostonian, after all. By October 2003, Ryan was a full-fledged member of the Nation, and he was thrilled that his favorite team was in the playoffs. My wife and I obliged by letting him stay up late to watch some of the playoff games. My favorite moment that month occurred right after Game 6 in the ALCS. I was enrolled in an evening course at a local college and a midterm exam had been scheduled for that class. Unable to see the end of the game, I called home as I completed the examination, and my wife answered. Before I could ask what had happened, she told me, "Your son is still up, and he has something to tell you." The joy in his voice was unforgettable as he shared the good news.

Naturally, Ryan was allowed to stay up late the following night to watch Game 7. And like many other parents in Red Sox Nation, the reward for my faith on that particular evening was to sit on the side of my child's bed and reassure him that there's always next year, as he fought back tears. I spent most of that night lying restlessly in bed, anguished over what had happened. I had truly enjoyed sharing those games with Ryan, and I genuinely worried that he would lose enthusiasm or even turn away from the Red Sox as a result of this bitter loss. But my fears were unfounded, and before long he and I were excitedly discussing the trade for Curt Schilling and looking forward once more. I am so proud at the strength of my son's belief in this Red Sox team during the past twelve months. Even though the team of choice among his New York state middle-school classmates is the Yankees, Ryan wears his Red Sox hat and SCHILLING 38, jersey without apology. I cannot thank this wonderful team enough for helping to forge an unbreakable bond with my son.

Most of all, win it for yourselves. "Why not us?", indeed.

—Jim Devlin

Win it for all the women in our lives who have cheered and suffered right along with us, become fans in spite of themselves, and who recognized the greatness of Big Papi long before we did. And for my dad, who, upon his long-awaited return move to New England in 1978, took his family, with almost nothing in the new house unpacked, to see the Sox beat George Brett and the Royals. You deserve it Dad. And for my Grammy, smiling up there somewhere, who still lusts after Ted Williams in her heart.

—FredCDobbs

Win it for my dad, James Carolan (1909-2000).

He saw Ruth pitch (live), and he saw Pedro pitch (on TV).

And now, he's upstairs playing gin rummy with Joe Cronin between games.

—Chris Carolan

Win it for ....

My late great-grandparents, Nana and Pa Joe Allander. They began rooting at a time when the Red Sox were regularly winning World Series titles, and were still listening and watching all the games in the late 1960s when I began my own odyssey. I wish they had lived a few years longer so that I could have talked to them more about the glory days of the teens.

My grandfather, Edward Armour. The last time I saw him he was in a hospital bed and I was on the way to Fenway Park with my brother and father, in the summer of 1975. We talked about the Red Sox, who were on their way to a pennant and great World Series. He missed both, but I cherish the games I was able to watch with him as a child.

My father. We used to make the trip once a year or so from Connecticut to Fenway Park, and Dad always made certain we got there hours early so that we could be there when the gates opened. Not just batting practice, we needed to watch the grounds crew put the lines on the field. Years later, when I was attending 20 games a year, I usually show up just in time for the first pitch, but once in a while I would stop to pay attention, to remember how I used to feel when I walked through the tunnel and spotted the green grass and heard the organ.

My mother. I suppose she put up with a lot, with me insisting we listen to the Red Sox on the car radio on all family trips, even during our annual Maine vacation.

And insisting that I watch the Red Sox on television when it was a sunny summer day. When I left Boston for Oregon in 1993, my mother seemed most shocked that I was leaving the Red Sox and Fenway Park. She was right. My family all left New England before I did, so the Red Sox truly have been the hardest part of my separation. I have watched baseball all over the country, and have written many words about the Red Sox in recent years, but I have never missed Boston as much as I do right now.

I can't quite go so far as to ask for myself. I have had my share of breaks over the years, so when good fortune is passed out I am willing to get in back of the line. Just win it for all us Red Sox fanatics. We have endured a lot, but we are all still here, and that is something.

—Mark

Win it for ....

Following a team is not supposed to hurt. By nature, sports are supposed to provide a pleasant diversion from the daily grind.... the opportunity to forget about your cares and worries, sit back, relax, and enjoy watching a game. In theory this is a great idea. I, however, was born a Red Sox fan, and have never felt carefree and worry-less when watching my team. I think that's what sets Red Sox fans apart from many other fans. Every team has its set of rabid fans.... the ones that live eat and breathe their squad. The Red Sox, on the other hand, seem to require such a following.... casual fans need not apply.

So what I want is for the Red Sox to win this world series for every fan who thinks that they are strange, different, god forbid stupid, for caring so much for a group of guys who play baseball. As a fan base we watch each game helplessly and surrender our hearts each day to the Sox. Should a baseball team determine how much sleep you get on nights without games? Should a baseball team be able to make the worst day of your life suddenly bearable because of a home run off of fruitbat? Should a baseball team make you spontaneously laugh or cry during a highlight reel montage? No, it should not. But the Red Sox do, and that's never going to change. So, I want the guys to win it for the people who get nauseous before big games, who pace in jams, who would give up personal gain or notoriety simply to have the Sox win the last baseball game of the season.

Just win.

—Brett M. McCartney

Win it for me.

1986 was the year my parents and I immigrated to Boston from war-torn Lebanon. I was 11 years old and only 3 months into my new life in the U.S. when the Sox and baseball helped me forget all the traumatic experiences of growing up in that ravaged country. Not realizing it then, the '86 Sox introduced me to what life is all about. I want us to win it for my brethren in Red Sox

Nation, so that we can experience the full gamut of what life is all about.

—Razmig Elmayan

Win it for my dad, who idolized Ted Williams growing up in his New Jersey neighborhood even though all the other kids rooted for Joe DiMaggio. Who would sit outside on the deck of our NJ home every night, fighting an old radio to get WTIC out of Hartford to come in through the static, and who made his kids Sox fans in the heart of Yankee country. He's 70 now, has the baseball package on his TV instead of an old radio, but still follows every pitch of every game.

For my mother, who doesn't understand baseball one lick, but understands the passion the men in her life have for the Red Sox all too well.

For my brother, who works in NYC and had to face the taunts and jeers of an entire city after Game 7 last year.

For my 7-year-old nephew, who had to unlearn his foot tapping wiffleball ways when his favorite player was traded earlier this year, and who still doesn't understand why the other kids in his NJ first grade class taunt him with "Red Sox suck!" May he have the last laugh this year.

For me, who had to go to school and face a legion of 6th grade Met fans he day after Buckner's boot.

For my pregnant wife, who somehow jumped up and down higher than me when her favorite player broke out of his slump and hit a grand slam in Game 7 to help beat the Yanks.

And finally, for my unborn child, who was there with us when the Sox finally won it, and who will grow up in a world where the words "Red Sox" and "Cursed" will never again be synonymous.

—Brian Perillo
Florham Park, NJ

Win it for ....

My grandfather Dean, who flew 44 missions as a B-24 tail-gunner over Europe in WWII. Although he was a Cubs fan, he liked the Red Sox as well and his favorite player was Ted Williams.

My dad, Jim, who pitched in college against Phil Niekro. He passed his love of baseball on to me. When my son was born on my 33rd birthday, my dad made us a gift of two of his most prized possessions: The Ted Williams cards—#1 and #250—that bookend the 1954 Topps Baseball Card set.

My daughter, Allison, who attended her first games at Coors Field this year and had her baseball autographed by just one Red Sox player, Derek Lowe.

My wife, Sonja, who cared nothing for baseball before last season but caught the fever during the 2003 Red Sox stretch run. She now watches every game and, kids permitting, every inning.

My son, Jackson, a two-year-old rookie in Red Sox Nation who cheers no matter what.

The 1986 Red Sox who brought me into the Nation during that summer between my junior and senior years in high school over half my lifetime ago.

Stonewall Jackson. Just 'Cause.

—Doug Stalnaker

Win it for my dad, Bob (1944-1992), who introduced me to the world and passion of Red Sox baseball. We were season ticket holders to the New Britain Red Sox for many years.

Win it for all the Sox minor leaguers that we knew. That we traveled to away parks to see. The greatest times my dad and I had were traveling all over the East Coast to see the Brit-Sox play. To Glens Falls, Pittsfield, Harrisburg, or Williamsburg.

Win it for Dana Kiecker and Jose Burriel who took the time to take a picture with me and it still sits on my mantle. Also, Dana Kiecker who went to lunch with me one time in Vermont when the Brit-Sox where playing the Vermont Reds. Two of the coolest moments of my childhood.

—Jonathan Rogg
(Swing and a drive)

Win it for ....

#1. Win it for a lifelong Royals fan—Special Consultant to Theo Epstein, Bill James! I'd argue that NO ONE has contributed more to this team than James and his ideas about baseball. I credit him with Schilling, Ortiz and Bellhorn, and maybe others, being Red Sox players. A man who 15 years ago tired of writing "Dear Jackass" letters finally got to see his ideas fully implemented. He's belonged in the Baseball Hall of Fame for more than a decade—thank goodness, now he also belongs in the Red Sox Hall of Fame! Bill, I know some of your assistants read SoSH—I hope you read this, and thanks!

#2. Repeating Shaun, win it for Johnny Pesky, the Red Sox manager for the first game I ever listened to, on Voice of America from Barbados (and we beat the Yanks 4-3 in 11 innings!). But especially win it for Johnny since this Series is against the Cards, and can help to dispel angst over the calumny about him holding the ball. And please, mediots, bring Johnny to the forefront of our consciousness over the next ten days!

#3. Win it for my great aunt Grace Reece, who was a huge Ted fan and took me to my first Sox game in 1964 (again we beat the Yanks!), and who died on Bicentennial Day in '76, after her heart was broken the previous year. And win it for her brother, Uncle Bobby (d. 1972), who was a Sox fan since their founding in 1901, witnessed in person Fred Snodgrass's muff, and explained so much about baseball to me when I first moved to Boston.

#4. Win it for all the SERIOUS Sox fans with whom I have shared conversations and analyses over the past 40 years, including Steve Marino, Tom Ela, Mark Ruben, Pete Malinowski, Sam Miller, Francine Davis (who gave me the ticket that allowed me, alas, to witness Bucky's HR from the back of the bleachers), Bob Bloomberg (with whom I've watched so many games since 1967) and all the SoSHers with whom I have savored this season.

#5. Win it for my sons, A.J. and Eric, to whom I've passed on my addiction, and my wife, Deb, who is, after this last series, now a diehard Pedro, Papi and Schilling fan, and who can now argue better baseball than any of the guys at her work!

**—Stephen Devaux
(DamonasaNomad)**

Win it for my grandfather, Walter Quigley, who grew up on the North Side of Chicago, who moved to Boston as a teenager as has yet to see either of his teams win it all. Win it for my grandmother, his wife, Verian, who passed away July of 2003 and isn't here to witness this, but is definitely looking down at us, smiling.

Win it for those, who down 3-0, still believed.

—Steve Eaton

Win it for ....

I don't have generations of Sox fans in my family, so:

Win it for every MFY hater.

Win it for SoSHers in and out of New England.

Win it for Spaceman so he can write another book.

Win it for everyone who wants to forget about Gump.

—sfip

Win it for a thirteen-year-old boy who decided to watch a game of not-quite-cricket on TV—the first baseball game ever to be shown in England.

Win it for the team that played that day, and for all the Brits who fell in love with baseball then.

Oh, the game? October 18, 1986 (though I didn't see it until the Sunday afternoon). Boston 1, NY Mets 0.

Until they invented this internet thing, it was nearly impossible to follow baseball from England; since then I've fallen in love again with the sport and the team.

And win it for Jim Rice, who scored the first run ever seen in England.

—Richard

Win it for ....

At 51, I'm so afraid to write in this column…. I feel the same way I felt before game 6 in '86 right now, except I can't keep food down. Nevertheless….

Win it for my best friend Larry. I've known Larry for about 15 years now, and he and I have shared pretty much every Red Sox "issue" during that time.

The reason I want to mention him—I went through a pretty bad time in my life about 5 years ago. I came pretty close to "moving on." Larry saw me through it. He pulled me out and helped me be able to make it one more day. And then another.

If it wasn't for him, the Red Sox wouldn't be 1 game away from "winning it all" in my lifetime.

Thanks Larry!

—rice not rose

Win it for my grandfather, Edward Guy, who is the eternal optimist and tells me every spring this is our year. Approaching 81, he never lost faith in the Red Sox. Win it for him because a Red Sox win might numb some of the pain of losing his wife of 59 years in August of this year. Win it for my grandma, Veronica Guy (1924-2004), who is looking down on us and wishing she could be with us to celebrate a WS victory. Celebrating is one of the things she did best. We miss you Nana and know you have something to do with this incredible Red Sox run.

Thank you very much.

**—Phil Murphy
(theemerald33)**

Win it for ....

First of all—thanks again to Jack for starting this amazing thread, and to all of the ever-expanding SoSH family. This is what friendship and teamwork are all about....

On that note, I wish to say win it for friendship; for the notion that 1+1 can be so much more than 2. These guys have repeatedly shown all year that they do this for each other; for the right reasons. They are an inspiration to so many. Thank you!

And, on a personal note, win it for my father. He's in Moscow right now, missing most of this historic Red Sox moment. He's the one who taught me the power of friendship and doing things for the right reasons. I wish we could be together for this, Dad. I love you.

**—Nathan White
(sticksnw)**

Win it for my 86-year-old Uncle Mac Goldberg, a life long, diehard who for me was the first "knowledgeable fan."

He's now spending his days in a Reno, NV, care facility. Despite his age and frailty, he's aware.

Win it for my mother, Eva Winneg, who when I called her from the stadium after game 7 was in tears because she was so joyful.

Win it for my buddy, Mark Kates. We met on Oct. 2, 1978 and attended our first Red Sox-Yankee game together on 10/20/04. When BFD threw out the first ball, we knew we had it in the bag. So devoted to the Sox is he that when he moved back east from LA to start his record label, he named it Fenway Recordings. In our Lifetime, Mark. In our Lifetime.

Win it for my brothers, Stu and Rob Winneg. We've been through it all.

Win it in memory of my late dad, Allan Winneg. While he may not be physically here—his love for this team has been passed to his boys and his spirit will be soothed.

Most importantly, win it for yourselves.

—Ken Winneg
(May468)

Win it for the chance to go to the world series. And then…. win that, too. Win it for us. Me and all of you, everbody mentioned. Win it for the older guys. Win it for all the people I was an @#%$ to when I took my frustrations out on them. I want to see how the people I love react the first time they see me. I want to know what I'm going to do when they win.

WIN IT FOR ALL THOSE MFY FANS THAT MAINTAIN THAT THEY WANT TO US WIN ONE IF THEY DON'T! I HATE THEM THE MOST!

—Hair and cheese

Win it for all those kids at Dana Farber and the countless charities that these players give their time for. Those children see the Red Sox as heroes in a way we can't understand. For them, a win tonight would certainly give them strentgh and inspiration. Win it for Jimmy.

—Jeff Goldberg
(Buffalo Head)

Win it for....

To name but three:

Win it for Johnny Pesky, win it for Bart Giamatti and win it for the old man at the bar, whispering: "We never should have taken out Willoughby."

Redeem them.

"somewhere I have never travelled, gladly beyond any experience, your eyes have their silence: in your most

frail gesture are things which enclose me, or which I cannot touch because they are too near."

—e.e. cummings

And win it for the fans in Red Sox diaspora all over the
world, who are sitting silently at home, living and dying
with each pitch, "shouting with joy in the middle of the
night over the haphazardous flight of a distant ball," and
enjoying our Red Sox with you, our brethren at Boston,
the living and the dead, in the green fields of the mind.

—carl-albert heller

Win it for Lou Thompkins, those of you fortunate enough to know
who he is will fully understand. For those of you who
don't, google his name, there is an entire Little League
organization named after him here in eastern
Massachusetts, and it is my firm belief that he has kept
more young kids out of trouble in the summer time than
anyone anywhere has done voluntarily.

Win it for my father who tirelessly taught me the game
that I came to love. The man who coached Little League
teams in a town which would not let you coach your
own children, just so he could keep an eye on his kid's
friends and make sure they didn't get into trouble. The
man who has given up on this team so many times, but
has fallen in love with them so many more times than
that. The man who can distinguish between a .225 hitter who runs through walls and .350 hitter that is a
prima donna and would take the lesser hitter every day
and twice on Sundays. The man who has passed his love

for this game to me for all the right reasons. The man who let me stay home from school after the 1986 series (I was 11) so we could practice grounders and take our minds off of the Sox together.

Thanks Dad, and I hope we get to see them win this one together....

Finally, thank you SoSH for the forum and all of RSN for being there not only for the team, but for each other. It is a sports bond that transcends the game, and it is unique and should be cherished. GO SOX....

—Deathofthebambino

Win it for my grandfather, Ben, who passed away a few days after September 11, thinking the world was a hopeless mess. Win it so that he can see how far we have come, and how so many things can be right with this world. Win it so he can see our future still looks bright, and that "inferior curse garbage" was, indeed, garbage.

Win it for the girl I was seeing who I made watch Game 7 of the 2003 ALCS with me. I wanted her to have the first Sox game she watched be the most memorable, but it was for all the wrong reasons. It was the first and only time she has seen me cry.

Win it for my grandfather, Roland, who watches all Sox games until "they start to lose." Hopefully he'll be watching for a long time now.

—Williams Head Case

Win it for .... Mabel Bagnell.

Diminutive in size, but as tough as nails. She took me in when I was very young in and raised me like one of her own. She loved the Red Sox with no reservations or expectations, through good times and bad times, and she passed on her pure love for the game to me. She died in 1985 and was buried with the hat of her beloved team on her chest.

I miss you, Granny....

—Chuck Korb

Win it for my Little League 'A' team coach, Scott. He is the first person who taught me how the game should be played and through him I learned of the joy and happiness of not only playing the game, but watching it, and even collecting baseball cards. He was always positive and always comforting, something especially important when you are dealing with 9-,10-, and 11-year-old kids. Living on the coast of Maine, Scott is a huge Sox fan and with this influence and that of my dad's, I have become a huge Sox fan my self. To this day I come home from college and talk to him about how the Sox are doing, about the last time we got down to Fenway Park, and how the high school baseball team will do this spring.

Today, 10/24/2004, as Scott was stuck in Boston on his way back from Florida (of course he wouldn't have minded watching Game 2 in a bar outside Fenway), he found out that his youngest son, Cameron, had had an accident today. His son, who was around 6 or 7 years old, had drowned in a gravel pit after running off from his grandmother while on an afternoon walk. A tragedy especially hard for a small island community. So win this for Scott, the biggest Sox fan I have ever met, and win it for his son, Cameron, who would have been as big of a fan if his dad had any say in it.

Also, win it for my summer league coach, Rich who was born and raised in Mass. A great teacher of the finer points of the game who instilled a hard nosed, gritty way of playing the game he loves so much. He would tell stories of growing up playing for Norwood in the summer leagues with future major leaguers and how he took a different path and enlisted for Vietnam. He loves the game, whether he is umping Little League games or talking with kids on the sidelines. Baseball has been a huge part of his life. He was there for the '75 World Series and he will be at home in Maine watching the game and team he grew up idolizing.

—Adam

Win it for ....

My wife. She didn't leave me when I told her that the Red Sox winning the World Series would be the single greatest moment of my life, besting even our wedding.

All the kids I knew growing up in Maine. We always talked about where we would be and how we would feel. I hope we'll know soon.

—James W. Warner
(MainerInExile)

Win it for my dad. He has been a lifelong Red Sox fan and never gave up. Being a doctor, he has helped so many people. It's his time to be helped out. He first introduced me to baseball with an old Red Sox cap. Although I was only 5 years old and the hat was way too big on me, I always wore it. He has had to put up with my constant Red Sox obsession for years now and he never complained once about it. Win it for my father because without him, baseball would just be a game to me. Just a silly game.

Thank You Red Sox.

—Liz

Win it for Marcia Smith, who at 81 years of Sox passion still has enough faith in the Sox to write her grandson a letter to lift his spirits and not to give up hope while they sat at 0-3. By the time the letter arrived to me in New York from North Kingston, RI, things had changed drastically and I look forward to writing her in return.

Most of all, win it for yourselves. Win it because your are the best team in the major leagues. You guys worked the hardest, you made us believers and every day you stepped on the field we knew we had a chance to win.

Win it because the entire nation is envious that you are our team.

Now, go out and win it!

—Andy Smith
New York, NY

Win it for my Pa. He died in 1988, and I have many memories of him on the porch in his home in Wareham, listening to the game, beer and cigarette in hand.

Win it for my Nana and Aunt Dotty. They both succumbed with in a week of each other, to cancer this summer. They leave behind a legacy of Sox fans. Such Sox fans indeed, that we all tried to encourage my uncle to go to the game the night of the funeral, to try to take his mind off things.

Win it for (AO, SF, DH, JR, MA, and AJ) my six Sox fan students who have followed my emotional highs and lows of the post season. They have been great in keeping me sane, and from yelling too much at the 22 other Yankee fans in the classroom.

Win it for yourselves. Win it for each other. Win, celebrate, and rejoice.

—curtsfan38

Win it for .... Father Paul. Father Paul is still with us (must be the clean living) but is in his late 60s. He is the parish priest at our church, St. Paul's in Austin, Texas, a looong way from the hub of the universe. He grew up in Quincy with three brothers but no dad, so the Red Sox were, at times, father figures to him. When my family first moved from New England to Austin, we certainly didn't expect to run into any Red Sox fans. Little did we know the reach of Red Sox Nation. Father Paul warmly greeted us upon our joining his parish but it wasn't until spring training rolled around that we grew to understand his passion for the Red Sox. He takes a week off annually to visit the Sox in Florida and always brings back autographs and other memorabilia to auction at the summer parish fair. Father Paul often weaves the Red Sox and Yankees into his sermons (typically "good versus evil" types). He regales us with stories of Teddy Ballgame or Yaz or Nomar. He even has NESN piped into his cable TV and has setup a mini Fenway Park in his yard. Best of all, he's bonded with my 7-year-old son over their love of the Sox and it's really helped my son come to admire Father Paul as a community hero.

—Michael Brucker

Win it for my father and my twin brother who have been devoted fans their whole lives. My father still won't talk about '86 except to say that it was the only night in his life that he did not sleep. He just sat in his chair all night and just stared. In all the time I have known both of them, I have never seen them go to bed without knowing the Sox score. Baseball and the Red Sox have always been a huge part of our family. I'm blessed to have watched the Sox with both of them. Greatest baseball fans I've ever known.

Win it for my sister-in-law's Uncle David who passed away on Christmas morning after knowing that, because of cancer, the 2003 season would be his last. He never missed a game and when cleaning his apartment after his death, they found an entire collection of Starting Lineup figures for the Red Sox. Even in his 60s, he was still a kid at heart.

**—Bill Bernier
(Makinaw Peaches)**

Win in for my grandfather who passed on to me his love of sports and the Red Sox. He never got a chance to see me play the game he loved so much or see the Red Sox win the WS.

Win it for my great uncle who has given over 60 years of his life to coaching and umpiring youth baseball doing his best to teach kids the "right way" to play the game. I'll never forget one his favorite sayings, "God gave you two hands to catch a baseball, not to suck an egg!" Not sure what it means but I find myself saying it every time Manny nonchalantly one hands one in left.

Win it for my girlfriend so she won't become the pessimistic fan that I am. Her childlike enthusiasm on our first trip to Fenway this summer when she bought an Ortiz jersey gave me hope that this year would be different.

Win it for the Sox of my youth who I spent countless hours mimicking in the backyard when I was growing up—Dewey, Pudge, Rice, The Can, Geddy, Rooster, Armas, Hurst, Steamer and most of all Yaz.

Win it for the voices of Red Sox Nation, Remdawg, McDonough and Orsillo, that should be there calling this series rather than those Fox phonies.

And lastly, win it for all of us Red Sox fans so that we may never again hear 1918 and shudder!

I believe!

—Andrew Smith

Win it for my dad, a lifelong Red Sox fan, so he'll stop being so damn negative and remember that keeping the faith always pays dividends. He wants his ashes sprinkled at Fenway Park so he'll be there if they finally win a title. Win it so that I never, ever have to go through with that.

Win it for Jonathan A. He may be blind, but he has been "watching" the Sox his entire life. After all of his struggles to overcome his disability, he deserves a World Series title.

And win it for this nineteen-year-old girl, who had her heart broken by Aaron Boone and the departure of Anthony Nomar Garciaparra. Perhaps a World Series will cure that broken heart at last.

Win it for Loopie.

—Chris Losch

Win it for ....

For my dead grandfather, William F. Donahue, who passed in '94. My earliest memories were sitting with him eating Breyer's Natural Vanilla ice cream on weekends at Salisbury Beach watching the Mike Greenwell-era Red Sox. I'm sure he's been watching NESN with the big guy upstairs since then.

For my other recently deceased grandfather and namesake, John Munro Jr. The only reason we wanted to keep his heart pumping the last few months as he died in a nursing home was maybe, just maybe, he could see his Sox win a World Series. He left us a couple of months too early, but it would make victory just as sweet.

The elderly Sox fan I hugged at Yankee Stadium on Wednesday night (ALCS Game Seven). Seeing the look of relief and jubilation on his face was one of the most emotional experiences I have ever been through for some reason. Baseball truly has the power to unite generations of complete strangers.

**—John Munro
(Alanembeer)**

Win it for my grandpa, who died five hours before game 1 of the ALCS against the Yankees. He was a father of 10 and grandfather of 26, who loved his grandchildren more than anyone I've ever seen. Nothing was ever out of the question when the grandkids were involved, whether it was buying one of those $300 kites, taking us out on his

boat, or building Pinewood Derby cars that would win every derby they were entered in, without fail.

He taught us all the meaning of a hard day's work as well. My brother and I would get up at 8 on Saturday mornings and go down to Grandpa's and mow the lawn, paint the deck, and move the occasional Japanese Dogwood across the lawn, always being paid just slightly below minimum wage. But we had fun, had a great lunch, and had a good time with Grandpa.

He wasn't the biggest Sox fan, but he would want to see them win because it would make me happy, and that was all that really mattered to him when it came right down to it. So win this one for Grandpa, who's looking down at Fenway now, making sure the Sox get the bounces and the wind picks up when it needs to, just to put a smile on my face.

—Seabass

Win it for the players who have come and gone from the system. For 1946, 1967, 1972, 1975, 1978, 1986, 2003, and all the other years where great teams and great players had just fallen short. For Tim Wakefield, a true Red Sox lifer. For Carlton Fisk, the ultimate "Yankee hater," for Dom DiMaggio, who should be in the Hall of Fame, for Nomar, who was the face of the franchise for several seasons.

Win it for my family who helped instill the love of the game inside me no matter how much I used to resist in my younger years. For my father who took me to my first baseball game in 1998 against the Royals. For my mother who told me stories about watching the '75 World Series with her friends and her love of Carlton Fisk. For my older sister who makes me look smart as a fan. More importantly, for my older brother, the biggest fan I know. He's a jackass at times, but he mostly made me the fan I am today. He quizzed me on statistics, told me whatever news he could, always had on *SportsCenter*, even when I didn't know the stuff he quizzed me on, I'd look it up and each day it'd help me become a smarter fan. For my uncle, who battled cancer in the past year, another great Red Sox fan that I know of.

Win it for those who believed in miracles. The ones who believed while being down 0-3 that maybe, just maybe, the Red Sox could overcome that obstacle and achieve the impossible dream. For the ones who were laughed at or yelled at for still believing, the ones who refused to see the reality and looked to the possibility. They're the ones who truly deserve it for their grace under pressure and thick skin.

Win it for the younger generation, so they don't have to go through the same oppression, pain, and waiting that the older generation had to endure. I was only a baby in 1986, but I've heard the stories time and time again and 2003 broke my heart. However, the younger generation who are the hope for the future of Red Sox Nation doesn't need that kind of oppression. Win it so they'll just think of 1918 as another year.

Win it to shut up the oppressors and critcs. For the ones who threw guys like Tim Wakefield, Bronson Arroyo, Curtis Leskanic, Mark Bellhorn, Bill Mueller, and Kevin Millar to the side, telling them that they weren't good enough to be part of a championship team. For the broadcast crews who criticized the way the team looked and the way they played. For McCarver and Joe Buck to shut up about the curse, which doesn't even exist.

Win it for my friends and co-workers. For my non-Red Sox fan friends whose hearts lie in allegiance for other baseball teams, who put up some interesting baseball debates with me throughout the season. For my non-baseball fan friends who had to put up with my bitching about how Jason Varitek shouldn't be playing during a day game, against Mike Mussina with the temperature below 70 degrees, well not that drastic but close enough.

Win it for my fellow Red Sox fan friends, whether I helped convert them or not, they're still true fans and they deserve to see a World Series championship more than me. Most importantly, win it for my boss at work, a true Red Sox fan. He's my one true confidant when it comes to Red Sox baseball. I can talk to him about the team and not feel like I'm an idiot. Sometimes, I'd just come in on off days from work to talk Red Sox baseball with him, just as long as I wasn't completely distracting him. I had some of the best discussions of baseball with him. My friends deserve this.

Win it for the nerds! The ones who toil for hours and hours about all these different random as hell stats about certain players. Their passion shouldn't ever got unnoticed.

Win it for yourselves, the 2004 Boston Red Sox. You guys are loud, crazy, dirty, insane, and just plain old whacked out. You gave us lots of moments of entertainment, on and off the field. Sometimes you made us want to kill you and call the season over, but you guys are truly one of the greatest Red Sox teams of all time and of my short but well-lived lifetime. You guys have shown me so much over this entire season. You showed me that even the little guys can contribute; you showed me that if you truly believe in yourself, you can do almost anything; you showed me heart; you showed me grit; you showed me the greatest miracle in baseball history. You guys truly deserved this World Series.

—Pine Tar Helmet

Win it for my dad, who was born in 1925 and died just 33 days ago. In the 40s he used to take his girlfriend—later my mom—to Fenway on dates.

—Pandemonium67
Tacoma, Washington

Win it for my father (1947-2002). The last Sox playoff game we were in the same room for was game 6 of the '86 series. I was in a hotel room on the way to basic training for game 7. Every 5 minutes I catch myself wanting to call him about this team, and every 5 minutes I remember he's gone.

Win this sunuvabitch, boys. Win it.

—Bergs

Win it for my Pepe, who was born in Dec. of 1918 and died in Nov. of 2002. A longtime Red Sox fan who always enjoyed Nomar and really enjoyed it when NESN became part of free cable a few years ago, he never got to see them win it all, but I know Chappy is rooting for them from his perch now. I thought of him often during the end of the Yankees series and how much he would have enjoyed it. Since they lived close by, I spent many Friday nights as an adolescent at my grandparents' house, and watched more TV38 games than I could count with him and my Meme and whomever else was there. He didn't join me when I went into the other room at age 11 to watch Roger Clemens' first 20 K game on scramblevision, but he was definitely one of the first ones I told of the result.

Win it for my great uncles, Phil, Ovey and Al. All three of them were big Red Sox fans who passed without ever seeing them win it all, and would often be there on the weekend at Chappy's for fish and chips or beans and then watching the game. Like my Pepe and Meme, they were not only fans of the team, but they were always the type of people whose kindness and generosity I will always remember.

Win it for my Meme, born in Oct. 1918 (just missed it by a month) and still kicking, even though she doesn't kick as fast as she used to. Despite not sharing the same intense interest in the team as her husband, brothers, and descendants, she never complained about any of us monopolizing her tv on Friday nights or Sat/Sun afternoons. Definitely the most loved member of my family, I won't hold against her the events of this past Saturday. Feeling bad karma emerging while I was at my parents' house in the 4th inning of Game 1 of the WS, I left for my apartment, but stopped by my grandmother's first to fulfill a promise to move a dry sink from one room to another. Of course my grandmother is there in the living room watching Navy NCIS, probably one of 100 people in the state of Mass. actually tuned in to CBS at that time. (I later reasoned that she was just avoiding McCarver for her health.) Despite some good natured ribbing about her tv viewing, she came out in the kitchen where my girlfriend Wendy and I had moved the dry sink, and she saw the kitchen tv that I had turned on to Fox approximately 8 seconds after my arrival at her house. She yelled out "7 to 5. They're winning!" but then appropriately qualified it 10 seconds later with a "oh my god, it's only the 4th inning." Thank god, she didn't see the number of errors. She'll be pleased with a win.

Win it for my dad, who took me to my first game against George Brett and the Royals at Fenway in the early '80s, and for my mom, who has put up with more heartbreak than any saint deserves. Earlier this past Saturday, I was home talking to them about the '86 Series and how I was looking forward to Game 1 that night, and I'm bringing up the story to Wendy about how my parents somehow got 2 tickets to the last World Series game the Sox had won at Fenway prior to the age of Bellhorn. [All this without ever entering a virtual waiting room for the tix.] My mother basically admitted that she couldn't even remember whom the Sox were playing in that Game 5 until I told her "Mets," but she did distinctly remember the obese man who sat next to her in the bleachers that night. (Upon my joking questioning, she stated that she was not referring to my father, whom she later qualified as "heavy, but not obese.") While this just gave me more ammunition for my long-standing argument of 18 years that I should have definitely attended that game instead of her, hey at least I still got the fat orange colored ticket stub sitting somewhere in my old bedroom. May my parents both get a well-deserved happy ending, and may I get the next WS tickets given to my family.

Win it for all my other relatives and friends, all the way down to my two nephews, Ryan and Aidan, ages 5 and 1½. The Red Sox have never lost a playoff series since I gave them their stylish Ramirez and Ortiz t-shirts in July, and they don't stop smiling. Perhaps they know something.

Finally win it for all the members of Red Sox Nation. Especially for the SoSH and all of its stars, ranging from the dopes to Rocco to Manila to G38 and a special shutout to the talented writer and peddler of jock paraphernalia, Jose Melendez. At my prior job in Boston, ESPN.com and *Boston Globe* sports and 98% of the sports websites were inaccessible to us office drones. However, I was able to access and use the *Atlanta Journal-Constitution* website to get live MLB scores

(Suck that tech support!), and me and a few other compatriots were able to successfully access the SoSH board. To me, SoSH was the key to really getting me through some tough days when I needed an outlet, a smile, news on an injury, an update on a day game, or a place to waste time. Heck even now, while at a better job, I still waste time there, even when I shouldn't.

One game left, time to get it done boys. Let's do it!

—Ctaffe

Win it for ....

For an 18-year-old fan in the University of Oregon student union—who learned on that fateful day 18 years ago what being a Red Sox fan really meant. *ouch*

For J.H.—somebody who comes by his love of the Red Sox more honestly than I (at least he grew up in Massachusetts), who has been a fan for longer than I, and who will (I hope) have something good to say this time!

For M.d'E.—a good friend—our shared love of the Red Sox (and Steelers!?) has made our friendship better.

For Wade Boggs. There are many Red Sox players I have admired over the years, but he was the very first baseball player that I noticed in a statistical way. Man I loved watching him hit!

And for all of us members of Red Sox Nation who are a long ways away from ground zero, and somehow got hooked anyway (we don't even have a decent excuse).

—Asoka Diggs

Win it for my grandmother, Josephine Patti; a lifelong Red Sox fan who came to this country from Sicily after WWI. In her later years, her favorite players were Ellis Burks and Nomar. She died just over three years ago at age 91 never getting to see her beloved Sox win it all (she was still in Sicily in 1918, and had no clue about baseball then). My grandmother loved the Sox.

So do I.

—Chris Patti

Win it for every soul in heaven who believed in a God. They believed in a God, and got to heaven at the end of their time. I find it ironic that Red Sox fans in heaven have had two distinct beliefs throughout their life, regardless their age; that the Red Sox would soon, one day, win it all, and that there is a higher power among us. Their belief in a God was ingrained in them as early as their belief in the Red Sox. We are to never know what belief was held stronger for those already in heaven, but we do know that after one more win, these things that are believed in with all of our heart, truly do exist. It is this belief, this faith, that the wishes of thousands of deceased Red Sox fans will now be complete, including two that I hold dear to my heart, Grampy Dave and Grampy Tom. God bless you, God bless us, God bless the Red Sox, and God bless wishes coming true, regardless of their expiration date.

—Anthony H. Melia

Win it for ....

* My grandfather Primo. I know he's watching from up above, the best seats in the house.

* My cousin Rob, who died in a car accident too young, eating cracker jacks next to Primo.

* My dad, who; I'm taking tonight; he's lived through the agony a lot more than me.

—David DeChellis

Win it for Malcolm Parker Trees (1917-1991) of Sudbury.

Win it for Lionel Montgomery Rodgers (1913-2001) of Norwalk.

My grandfathers loved baseball, Boston, and the Sox. Much of Mal was left on Guadalcanal after he stitched up and picked up too many parts of Marines, but he could always relate to someone over the Sox. When I was a little kid, the first thing Lionel would do every day when we were visiting was read the game story out loud over breakfast to us.

Let's do this.

For Elizabeth Rodgers, my daughter. Born 12:21 A.M., October 28, 2004. She's never known anything but a Sox dynasty.

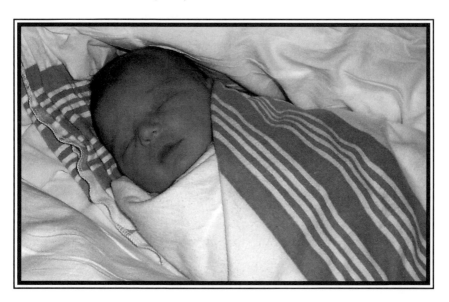

**—Owen Rodgers
(Dlew On Roids)**

Win it for ....

It was announced on October 20th that the company I work for was acquired. I thought when the Red Sox won the 7th game on the same day, that this was a VERY good sign for our company. Most of the folks here are huge Red Sox fans and were elated Thursday morning.

This morning 20% of us were laid off. Thankfully, I still have a job but I really really want to win the World Series for the Red Sox fans who were laid off today.

Go Red Sox!

—Lefty on the Mound

Win it for ....

Wow.... um.... let me try to get through this.

Win it for Courtney Odell.

I moved down here, to North Carolina from New Jersey, one year ago this month, to get a fresh start. In fact, I was driving down with all my stuff in the car the night the Marlins won the World Series.

And, well, this past year has been a pretty trying year, as I've gone through it getting my life back together after some years of, bluntly, f***ing things up and having a bad string of missed opportunities and setbacks.

I hit a point back in March where I was at the low point in my life. So-called "family" in NC saying things and doing things behind my back, all alone down here without anyone, anyone who cared about me at all, my parents, a good 600 miles away. I was sick with a horrendous flu. Miserable weather. Bad.

Then I found a voice....

I had just gotten my current job as all this was happening, but I had to delay my start date for a good week because of my flu, and every day, living with my miserable "family," I called in every morning or got called every morning by this wonderful woman, the one lone voice anywhere near that gave two sh*ts about how I was doing, and we talked.

Five to 10 minutes every morning for a week straight, getting updates, just keeping in touch with the job, asking how things are, the basics.

Hadn't met her yet, since she had just taken over for the woman that hired me.

Got healthy, went to work, finally met her…. astonishing beautiful woman. Floored.

Next couple months I got to know her, finding out pieces of her story…. and I fell for her, yet for some ungodly reason I could never pull the trigger on asking her out. Unexplainable.

Then one day in June I found out she was moving, and moving fast. Her divorce went final; she had good friends in SC who hooked her up with a job; she was going to get her own fresh start.

Crushed.

….

Gave her a card that last final time I saw her. I told her that I'll never forget her, and that one day, someway, somehow, somwhere, I'll see her again.

Hugged, kissed, goodbye....

On this, the precipice for a nation of people, myself included, who've gone through the struggles, the tribulations, the ups, the downs, the sorrows, having this baseball team mirror their life, hoping to finally break through.

Hoping to finally overcome the odds.

Overcome the ridicule.

Overcome the missed expectations.

Overcome all the odds and finally, finally, in the eyes of everyone, come out on top, and fulfill the promise that was seen in them a long time ago, and see the light.

She was my light here in NC, and I'll never forget her. Never.

Win it for Courtney Odell.

Thanks.

—Paul J. Kobylarz

Win it for my great-grandmother, who would never miss a game when I was a kid…. straight off the boat Swede, but she just loved them to death.

She showed me early on that it's ok for girls to love baseball.

—Jneen

Win it for ….

I want the Sox to win it for my father. My father always had a quiet confidence in the Sox, even when they did not deserve it.

He took me out to Game 3 of the ALCS, flying cross-country. He wanted that to be something I'd always remember. I was 13.

I was inconsolable a few days later, and I was ready to turn off the 1986 ALCS in Game 5 when the 9th started. My dad told me to wait. "Just watch," he said. And of course, Baylor homered and Hendu became a cult hero.

During Game 6 in Shea, my father was playing poker with a bunch of Mets "fans" (our area has the Mets AAA team). When the Sox took the lead in the 10th, with that same quiet confidence, he stood up and told them, "Goodnight boys. I'm walking home. I'll be there in time to see the 3rd out. When you see me tomorrow at work, the Sox will be champs."

That 3rd out never came.

I want that 3rd out this year. He won't whoop and yell. There won't be tears of joy. He's just not that way.

But he will be happy. And he should be.

**—Derek Stewart
(DJnVa)**

Win it for ....

For Pa, who attended Game 1 with me Saturday night, but now lies in critical condition at Rhode Island Hospital having suffered not one but two heart attacks this morning. Please hang on....

It's amazing how fast you can be brought back to earth at a time like this. It's very surreal. He had the time of his life Sat night, luxury suite for the WS, a win for the hometown team, doesn't get any better (except if you're sitting in the dugout). And now he's fighting for that life. Trying to make him smile a little I told him he's supposed to have a heart attack AFTER something bad happens to our beloved Sox!

UPDATE: Pa pulled through and is doing just fine, and of course our beloved Sox won it all!

**—Steve Martin
(SteveSox)**

Win it for Al Hirshberg, writer for the *Boston Post, Boston Traveler,* and *Boston Herald,* author of many baseball books including *Fear Strikes Out,* who passed away in 1973. Al was my uncle and taught me to love baseball and especially the Red Sox. He lived and died with them yearly, from traveling to Florida to cover spring training through his coverage of the World Series. Although he only got to see Red Sox twice in the Series, he never lost hope that they would get there again and eventually win. I remember the many times that I would go to Al's Brookline apartment and walk with him to Fenway Park, where he would take me with him through the press entrance and then into the clubhouse or the press box. He seemed to know everyone, and everyone knew him. I used to hear many stories about players and about traveling to the various major league cities. Win it also for his wife Margie, her sister Bea Brown and her husband Cy Brown, my parents, all of whom shared Al's love for the Red Sox and helped instill it in me. Were they able to be here today, they all would be as thrilled as I am to have another opportunity. This time we cannot let it pass by.

—Geoff Brown

Win it for ....

My dad, Big Jim Bennett, who has been haunted with unconditional love for this team since '46. He recalls that Harry Brecheen was the most graceful pitcher who ever lived and he cannot utter the name Enos Slaughter (or Eddie Lopat) in a way acceptable in polite company.

My mom, who has been playing bridge for 40 years and never won a single time. She has no concept of or care for winning, but she loves the game and knows a good team when she sees one.

For Tony C. who taught kids of our generation that talent and life are beautiful, but fleeting things.

—Jim Bennett Jr.
(Vermonter-At-Large)

Win it for ....

My grandfather (1907-1997) who in his younger days used to go to the games and as he got older still watched on tv, always adding his own commentary. He is smiling down on us now.

All of us who have logged more hours sleeping on Landsdowne St. these past few weekends than we have in our beds. The sweet reward was being able to witness the energy inside the park during this great run and have amazing stories to share.

All the kids who are up way past their bedtimes and the teachers who are so patient with them in school.

All of us who believe in a higher power, in ourselves and in our team.

All of us who have achieved goals that others thought were impossible, who have persevered in the face of adversity.

—Marisa McQuaid

Win it for ....

.

My grandfather, who would listen to the games on the radio, even though he could have watched the games on TV. To this day I almost prefer listening and picturing in my mind what the action is....

My father, who I am POSITIVE thought that he would never see the Sox win it all....

For me, because I live and die with the Red Sox....

And finally, win it for my son, who was born on October 20, 2004—the day that we finally beat the Yankees.

Please win one more game.

—Glenn Strout

Win it for my dad. My baseball buddy who loved analyzing each move and saw things so clearly. Win it for me and my brother who are teaching our kids to root for the Sox and who have leaned on each other so much since our dad passed away Oct. 1, 2002.

Win it for all of the current and past Sons of Sam Horn and Dickie Thon Fan Club members. This is what it's all about. Rooting for our team and commiserating with our online friends.

Win it for the loyal fans of the Boston Red Sox. We're rooting for you and know that you'll give it your best tonight. That's all we ask.

**—Reuben Cochran
(Montana Fan)**

Win it for ....

Win this for my Puppy (my grandfather, Bobby Shelan) who died at 83 last week, having never seen a championship. He used to ask me every year if I had my World Series tickets, and if I would take him if they made it, I just want to tell him that I have my tickets this year and he will be there with me in spirit. Thanks, it felt great to get this out!

—Windycitysoxfan

Win it for ....

I want the Red Sox to win it for my grandfather William Ashline. He died in 1980 when I was in college. He lived in Acton, Mass., and was a devout RS fan. I have vivid

memories of him sitting in his kitchen (after my grandmother died) on summer nights, drinking Bud in a glass
and listening to the games on AM radio with Ned
Martin doing the play-by-play. He never saw them win
the WS but he always was there for them I have been a
Sox fan since '67 and I feel he is responsible. I always
think of him when the Sox are in the postseason and
wish he could be here to experience the winning of it all.

—RSTarheel

Win it for ....

I would like to add a couple people. First is my great
uncle, Eddie Pellagrini. Born on March 13, 1918, in
Boston, MA; the same fateful year the origination of a
mythical "curse" began. As a professional baseball player,
he was a journeyman. He began his career in 1946 with
the Boston Red Sox. The hometown kid was a utility
infielder, playing in 25 games at shortstop and third
base. Teammates and later best friends (until his passing)
with the great Ted Williams and Johnny Pesky, (whom
he served as understudy to mostly) he was party to the
crushing game seven World Series defeat at the hands of
the Cardinals. He says he still feels the pain of that defeat
to this day.

He left the Sox after the 1947 season, and went on to
play for 4 other teams during his eight-year career,
including the St. Louis Browns, Philadelphia Phillies,
Cincinnati Reds, and finally Pittsburgh Pirates. Branch
Rickey wanted him to manage his Pirates after he retired
in 1954, but he turned that down to return to his native

Massachusetts and beloved Red Sox, where he continued to support his first and only hometown team to this day. He went on to become the head baseball coach at Boston College for 31 years (1957-88), where after a few years of retirement, the "Eddie Pellagrini Baseball Diamond" was named after him.

He was the "little man" so often referred to, yet so quickly forgotten amongst the stars. The Rickey Gutierrez of the teams that win (or lose) and we never remember years down the road after the dust settles. Well I for one would like to take this opportunity to thank him and all the rest of the "little" men out there. They are as big a part of this to me as the Ted Williamses, Carl Yastrzemskis, and other stars of the past and present. Win it for the "little guys"!

Also, let's add the late Ray Boone, and all the countless others who have passed on after a life of hopes, prayers, and devotion to this team and its fans. Win it for them.

And lastly (and since it's a bit dusty here now), win it for my Little League coach who taught me everything about baseball on and off the field. He taught me to play fair and have fun, and cultivated my passion for the Red Sox. The countless phone calls back and forth whether it be the Hot Stove Season, or the middle of a game, the Red Sox have always been a constant in our lives. There is no way to describe or repay such a feeling or the great ride it's been, regardless of seasons past outcomes. The flame burns forever strong. Thanks Dad, this one's for us!

—Daniel McNaught

Win it for:

All of us too close to forty New Englanders who grew up listening to Ned Martin and Jim Woods call the Red Sox on that old AM radio.

For my dad, who was a Dodger fan until they left for the West Coast and who taught me how to hate the Yankees.

For my daughters, who already have the unquestioning faith that only true Red Sox Fans can possess.

For Yaz, Lynn, Rice, Pudge, Dewey, Boomer, The Rooster, El Tiante and all of the Sox heroes of my youth.

For Wakefield, who should have been the MVP of last years ALCS.

Win it for Mrs Yawkey who was waiting in the clubhouse in Shea in '86, only to have to leave without celebrating.

Win it for everyone in Red Sox Nation, wherever they are, who know better than anyone on the planet what disappointment is.

Win it for Cubs fans, so they know too that anything is possible if you keep the faith.

Win it for the sheer joy of hearing all those promoters of the curse eat LOTS of crow.

Win it for all of us grown men who will be crying like babies when it happens.

GO SOX!!!!!!!!!!!!!!!!!!

—AC Spectre

Win it for ....

Harry Frazee so his name may no longer be tarnished by those who do not know nor seek truth.

Former Red Sox General Manager Dan Duquette, who laid the foundation for the 2004 Boston Red Sox.

Theo Epstein, who, born and raised a Sox fan, built on that foundation and completed the work.

Massachusetts Attorney General Tom Reilly, to show him that some bag jobs, even those concerning the ownership of the Boston Red Sox, do have happy endings.

Mark Bellhorn, Bill Mueller, Kevin Millar, Pokey Reese, Bronson Arroyo, and Gabe Kapler, misfits and castoffs from lesser teams who were told in one way or another they weren't champion-quality ballplayers before coming to the Red Sox.

Curt, Pedro, Wake, Lowe, and Foulke who have pitched with their hearts, souls, guts, and have gone above and beyond the call of duty, doing everything in their power to deliver Red Sox Nation to the promised land.

—Thomas J. Schnorrenberg

Win it for ....

I've not been as active a contributor as I would have liked this year, but I've been a constant reader and I feel bound to everyone in this thread. I've spent the last two hours, since the final out settled in Mientkiewicz's glove, alternating between laughing joyfully and maniacally, and sobbing uncontrollably. I suspect I don't have to explain these emotions to anyone here, and I doubt I COULD explain them to anyone who hasn't been through these wars.

My grandfather was a diehard Red Sox fan who passed away seven years ago without ever seeing his beloved team win the big prize. I know he's seeing it today. This one's for you, Pepere.

My mother-in-law died three years ago, after a long life as a Yankee fan. But I know she's smiling, too…. the people she loved were always more important to her than the teams she loved, and watching me bound through the house screaming tonight would have thrilled her to no end.

My father is about a thousand miles away right now. He might be asleep. He might not be, yet. I bet he heard my screams of joy before we even picked up the telephones!

I never thought I'd get to share this moment with you, Dad. Can you believe it???

And finally, for my son…. you're only seven, Adam, but I'm happiest of all for you. The absolute joy we shared tonight just might be a once-in-a-lifetime experience, but you and I can forevermore venture proudly into Yankee Stadium, with our heads held high and our "2004 World Champions" t-shirts displayed for all to see and envy. Whatever else happens in future years, we'll always remember the summer…. and especially the fall! ….when we vanquished the ghosts, exorcised the demons, and carried home the big prize.

—Rob Lamoureux

Win it for all those and more, but most importantly win it for yourselves—you've worked too damn hard and gone through too damn much to finish as another footnote in the historical Yankees abstract.

**—Andre Motuzas
(Lithuanian SoxFan)**

Win it for all of us members of the Nation stuck deep in enemy territory who kept the faith and braved the streets of Manhattan decked out in full Red Sox regalia that Sunday afternoon when, down 3-0, things looked their bleakest. Win it for the stares of mockery and pity we endured walking the streets of New York. Win it for the fellow Sox fan who walked by me that day in the West

4th subway station, proudly sporting a cap emblazoned with that comforting B, who simply said, "This is the year."

Win it for my mom (Sherry Berson Moss Holstein), a diehard, who manages to find a way to bring up Ted Williams in every conversation she's in. She sent me the following when she saw this thread. Win it for her and for everyone else who has worshipped at the altar of the most Splendid of Splinters.

I've read about four pages and am in tears. It makes me think of my father (Jacob Berson from Portland, Maine). I wish that my father, your grandfather, whom you were named after, were alive; this would make him so happy. I remember listening to the games on the radio with him and watching whatever teams were playing on television, after we got one (1955). He taught me to love the Red Sox. I remember how at the beginning of every season, he would stand holding the schedule and order tickets for him and me to see a Yankee game in August. This was for many years the day I most looked forward to all year. We would take the bus or train (from Portland) to Boston, ride the "trolley" to Fenway Park, and sit somewhere on the third base side. I felt so important and proud to be going with him. So, that's my memory. I really hope that they win this year, so I won't have to worry about not living to see it.

Win it for the Faithful.

—Jacob Moss

Win it for my dad. God I love him and miss him. The only thing that would make all this better is if he were here to share it.

Win it for my three kids, Maggie, Katie, and Joey. Not only did I have the joy of sharing the Sox with my dad, but now I know what it was like for him sharing it with his children.

Win it for Robinson Checo.

Many thanks....

—Rick Perreault

Win it for my mother, Roxanne Gibson, who passed away two years ago from breast cancer, and was a lifelong Red Sox fan. She too was the person that brought me to my first Sox game at Fenway Park, and turned me into a lifelong Red Sox fan.

**—Al Gibson
(agibson2000)**

Win it for my grandfather (9-5-03), who made sure we were raised right by sharing his great love of the game with my brother and me. He grew up in Brooklyn a Dodger fan, adopted the Mets when the O'Malleys skipped town, and converted wholly to RSN when his daughter started raising boys in Boston in the 1970s. He loved Pedro, says he never saw better. Better even than Koufax.

He so would love this.

**—Andrew Kaplan
(SteamersLament)**

Win it for Aunt Ruth in Braintree, for Aunt Fran and Uncle Al in Fitchburg, and for the rest of the family that grew from that small house on Day Street in Whitman. Especially

win it for Pop in Morris, N.Y., who took me to Fenway more often than I can recall. I'll never forget the night our standing room tickets parlayed into great seats against the Yankees, or the stacks of plastic cups (still in use 20 years later) we collected in the bleachers during an Orioles weekend series. And win it for the memory of Pop's father, who always knew just how to get to the ballpark: "Follow the Crowd!"

Thanks a lot. Now let's win this thing.

—John Harrington

Win it for my dad (1946-1998) who took me to a pair of Red Sox games at Fenway each September in the early '80s. He would pick me up at the end of school on Friday, and we'd drive from western Mass. to Boston in time for a 7:35 start. On Saturday we would go to the afternoon game and return home. In 1986 we were lucky enough to go to Game 7 of the ALCS together.

Win it for my sister (1970-1989) who went with me to Game 3 of the 1986 World Series.

—Bill Thieriot

Win it for ....

My dad died on August 4th of this year. He'd have been so thrilled to see the Sox come as far as they have. Even more important to him would have been to see how much happiness, excitement, and pride this team has brought to his son.

I miss him terribly.

Win it for my dad.

P.S. Win it for my daughter and my wife who've had to put up with my crankiness whenever the Sox lose.

—Daniel Reichert

Win it for ....

Win it so that my family can lay the next day's newspapers at the graves of two lifelong Red Sox fans.

One died not long after 1967. He was a fun-loving, faithful guy who worked summers as an usher at Fenway and who always teared up during the national anthem. The day the '67 Sox clinched the pennant he held up the homemade sign in center field that read "This IS Next Year."

The other died last May. He once was a lot like the first guy, but he became a pessimistic, brokenhearted old man. Yet he and I watched every game, every summer. Deep down the son-of-a-bitch still loved the Red Sox, he just wouldn't let you know it.

Win it for my mom, who leapt with me and Hendu in '86, and the next week had to give back all the congratulations in Atlantic City and tend to a heartbroken fat kid when she got back.

Win it for me, so I can get on with my life.

Win it for all the lifers and losers in RSN.

—Paul Chandler

Win it for this team. Nobody knows where the foundation of our team will be in a few weeks, but for now they are a perfect group of guys who clearly love each other and the game so much. It will be sad to see the last game this year

end and know that the team will not be the same next year, it is sad to think that last night could have been the last time Jason caught Pedro in a Sox uniform, and tonight could be a last for Derek Lowe. But that is why we have to win it now—for the 2004 Boston Red Sox. Winters are lonely when the Sox stop playing, but this year's team can live forever.

And win it for those of us who felt our first heartbreak at 12:16 a.m. on October 17, 2003. We came of age in the wee hours of that Friday morning, and while we haven't done the time that so many of you have, win it for us so that heartbreak may be our last.

Win it for all the kids who have ever gone through the Jimmy Fund and looked to the Sox for joy.

Win it for everyone who's ever loved the Boston Red Sox.

—Trude Raizen

Win it for ....

70 years of rooting for this team has taken its toll on my dad. Win it for him and for all the other moms and dads and grandmothers and grandfathers who have harbored some form of faith over the course of their long lives.

Sometimes, faith is rewarded. Let this be one of those times.

—Jack Brohamer Experience

Win it for all the great friends I made living in Cambridge 2002-2004. They greeted me with open arms and helped open the eyes of an ignorant European to the great game of baseball and the Red Sox in particular. Before I came I had never watched a baseball game.... now I'm up at weird hours, glued to MLB.tv. Thank you guys!

—Mads

Win it for ....

You probably all know that I dedicated this season and my sig to my mother's father, Charley Weir, who first saw the Sox in 1916, as a 9-year-old. He passed in 1972, and loved the Sox to the last day. He pitched a complete game win at the VFW Auxiliary picnic, but stayed up to watch the game that night. He put the "indigestion" off on the potato salad, and it turned out to be a massive coronary. Oh, and just to quell a nasty rumor—he did NOT brush back a 62-year-old lady!!!

(She was crowding the plate, so he clipped her on the a**.)

This is all I can think of when anyone quotes Petey about the Babe. LOL! Win this for me and my son, who is 20 now. The first time we walked down Landsdowne, gawking at the Monstah, we piled into the first parking meter in the line; 30 years apart, almost to the day.

It's so good to belong to RSN. Thanks for all the memories! (Pain, too, but as Gramp says, that's baseball, and there's always next year.) Here's to a history-making bunch of idiots.

Oh, one more guy; Mr. Emerson, our junior high principal, who not only set up a TV in the auditorium, but winked at any kid that wanted to sneak out of class to watch in '67.

—Charley Weir

Win it for....

For our fathers.... for our sons.... and for us.

**—Skip Desjardin
(Carmen Fanzone)**

Win it for.... so many people, including my mom, Mary Manfra, who died of lung cancer on 7/9/03, and who loved to declare "They're gonna lose" (just to taunt the rest of our family), while inside rooting wildly for them to win. I cried when Nomar was traded, not because it wasn't time for him to go (sadly, it was), but because it was the loss of another link to Mom, who would call me whenever he did something spectacular in a game. I can still hear the joyful excitement in her voice on the phone: "Did you see that? Nomar hit a home run!" "Yes, Mom. I saw it." :)

I truly believe that she and all the Sox fans in this thread are helping to make this happen, and that she still sends me joyous baseball moments. On Mothers' Day, 2004, I sat in the stands with my brother-in-law, (who lost his mom in '03 too), asking, "Mom, do you know I'm here?" just as the game began. First pitch, Johnny Damon hits a foul ball right to us. Coincidence? Maybe, but I'd rather think not....

Win it for our loved ones, here or departed, for our team, and for all the great people on SoSH.

—Carol Ryan

Win it for my grandfather who passed away in '94.

Win it for my grandmother who passed away in '02.

Win it for my dad who is a casual Sox fan but has been riveted by this postseason so far.

Win it for my mom who used to listen to Sox games on a little radio from Michigan late at night when I was a child. For the person who has always had that Sox obsession since she moved to the U.S. in 1973. For the person who cried with me in 1986 and felt the devastation of 1975, 1978 and 2003 as well.

Win it for Marissa Ann, who is cheering on the Sox in her mommy's belly and will be born in December. I like to think she is bringing the Sox some of this Karma.

Win it for my wife, Julie. She isn't necessarily a Sox fan, but she has stood by my obsession, has taught me to think positive over the last couple of years and even brought a victory Boston Cream Pie before Game 7 because she just KNEW the Sox were winning Game 7.

Win it for that little boy, who at the age of 4 went to his first game at Fenway Park and lost his voice screaming for the Sox from the right field seats against the Yankees. For the teenager that cried his eyes out on that fateful night in 1986 and for the man that just stared at the television in utter disbelief on October 16, 2004.

Win it for all the great former Sox who never felt that ultimate moment in a Sox uniform.

Win it for all of us.

—Gary Parker
(Sox Fan in Fla)

Win it for my father, David Johnson, who taught his daughters that sports, especially baseball, are not gender specific. My father's love of baseball infiltrated all aspects of our childhood. There was no escaping Eddie Andelman's talk radio, the Saturday afternoon games on TV, or the summer long game our family played against in the backyard, each night after supper. But we weren't looking to escape. At a very young age, we fell in love with the Boston Red Sox because our father loved them.

In the five years since my father's death, my sisters and I have continued to love the game and the team our father introduced us to, but without much thought given to how or why this passion developed. It all came together for us on a cold, wet night this past September in the Bronx. The Sox came from behind late in the game and my sisters and I screamed loudly, while praying silently that the Sox would be victorious. "We are all here together; loving this team; and enjoying Dad's legacy. We'll win," my sister said to us. We all knew it was true.

Thank you to the 2004 World Champion Red Sox! Thank you reminding us all, that those that we've loved and lost are with us all the time.

—Rebecca Johnson

Win it for Danny. The impressionable 15-year-old boy who cried the night away on October 25, 1986, after the ball skipped through Billy Buckner's legs.

Win it for Dan. The young adult who suffered the sweeps in '88, '90 and '95, and the disappointment of the failed runs of '98 and '99.

Win it for Dan. The 33-year-old guy who cried the early morning hours away on October 17, 2003, after the ball sailed into the night off Boone's bat.

Win it for me.

—Dan Pagano

Win it for my parents and older brother, all of whom passed away before I could share a Red Sox World Series win with them.

Win it for Dad so I can tell my children once again about him spontaneously pouring a beer over his head when the Sox clinched the pennant in 1967.

My dad brought me to my first game when I was four years old and made sure we got to Fenway a few times each year, no matter what our financial situation was. He loved the Red Sox and, had the Sox held on in 1986, I and my two brothers would have joined him for the reenactment of the beer shampoo.

None of my children ever met him but tonight, or whenever we win this thing, I will carry on the beer shampoo tradition for him. And I will feel, in re-telling the 1967 story to my kids, that they will know him in some way too.

Win it for my mom who never missed a single Little League or Babe Ruth game in which I played and who grew to love the Red Sox simply because her kids did. Ever the optimist, she would have been the one telling us not to lose faith when the Sox were down 3-0 to the Yankees.

Win it for my older brother Tony who suffered from multiple sclerosis for the last 20 years of his life. He taught me how to play sports when I was young (he was 11 years older than me) and more importantly he taught me to compete and to respect the game. Every coach I ever played for praised me for being coachable and being willing to give everything I had to be the best I could be. Tony taught me that.

I've taught my two oldest (and will teach my youngest) the very lessons he taught me. Every time a coach compliments them on their attitude and effort I smile. Tony lives on in them and each time I watch them compete in a game I think of him.

My 15-year-old son and he developed a very special bond. I know he too will be thinking of Uncle Tony tonight.

Finally, win it for my wife and kids who are the ones who must put up with my obsession with the Red Sox. My wife (then girlfriend) and I watched the 1986 World Series together and have shared so much since that day. She is the one person in the world who will truly understand what this World Series win will mean to me.

—Chuck Mosca

Win it for George Popowich (1927-2000), from Rochester, NY, who took his thirteen-year-old son to his first major league game, not to Cincinnati where his boy wanted to go to root on his beloved Rose and Bench, but to Fenway Park, where upon his son fell in love with Yaz, Lynn, Fisk, and all-things-Red Sox, not least of which their rabid fans, and so rooted on his new-found American League team along side his longtime National League Big Red Machine. The year? 1975.

A magical summer, watching your two teams battle all season and then meet in the Series. While my love of the Reds waned over the next few years, my love of the Sox only grew. I even had to move to New England to get closer to them. That summer of '75 made me a life-long fan of the game, generally, and a permanent member of Red Sox Nation, specifically.

My dad was a pretty funny guy when it came to baseball: he was not so much a Red Sox fanatic, but a Yankee-hater. In Rochester, NY, you can't get the Sox games on TV, so he would watch the Yankees nightly, rooting for whomever they were playing. You'd hear him down in our basement family room swearing at the television. I can only imagine his euphoria over the Sox victory in the ALCS and, of course, the manner in which they defeated the Yankees.

Dad, thanks for giving me baseball. You should be here!

Go Sox!!

—Daniel Popowich

Win it for ....

Win one for the late Pete Runnels, 2004 Boston Red Sox Hall of Fame inductee, and probably one of the most underappreciated Red Sox players of all time. He was down with OBP before OBP was cool. I fungoed many rocks after announcing his name, and imitating his swing.

My first hero, and first vivid Red Sox memory—pure joy and hometeam pride as I sat with my Gramp Harold Severance in Bangor, Maine, and watched Pete homer in one of the 1962 All-Star Games. And my first heartbreak—learning that he had been traded to the Colt .45s for Roman Mejias. Oh well, Yaz would win the Silver bat the next year, and Tony C. showed up the year after that.

This one's for you, Gramp.

—Sean Carroll
(Carroll Hardy)

Win it for my precious mother, whom I lost tragically in a car accident three years ago this month. I doubt that there was a day in her life when she could have named more than three players on the Red Sox, but since I was five years old, she always let me stay up past my bedtime to watch the Sox games, which allowed me to cultivate my passion for this franchise. There is a piece of her in the joy that this team brings me.

—John Camillus
(Mister Roper)

Win it for my father, Joe Stanton Sr, and my son, Patrick. My father has been rooting for the Sox since the early 1940s and he passed his love of the Sox on to his four children, who now have their five children hooked on the Sox and this playoff run. He has always believed and hoped that he will see the Sox win the Series, and now we will see it together. He taught us the fundamentals of the game, coached us in Little League, and he just met his 1940s boyhood idol Bobby Doerr at Game 2 of the World Series, and afterward, by chance, he sat with his daughters, Catherine and Joanna, above Doerr's retired number in the new right field seats.

Win it for Pesky, Doerr, Dom, Ted, Yaz, Fisk, Boggs, and Oil Can, and every other player and fan for the past 86 years who has never doubted the Sox will win it all.

—Joseph Stanton Jr.

Win it for everyone in New England who remembers a day like this with our dad.

Driving in from the North Shore with my dad for a "night" game, the name night game always gave me chills as a kid.... the approach from the Tobin and on to Storrow and then seeing the Citgo sign are deep memories.... the walk from the old night club disco parking lot over to the bridge with the smells of the square.... The approach up the bridge over the pike and the first view of the Monster.... turning the corner to hear the ol' carnival barker saying Piiistaashioooos peeeenuuuts.... Piiistaashioooos peeeenuuuts!!!!!!! The smell of cigars as you enter in to the park combined with the peanuts and the hot dogs.... the old ice cream bars.. grass green green green and the shine of the lights off the batting helmets.... The jerseys of our team the color of white that shined brighter with the huge light towers from above.... Sherm announcing the anthem and the echo of Yaz's name when he came to the plate that we all tried to imitate in wiffleball games at home with Ned on the radio in the side yard…. We settle in and Dad helps me score the game…. Boomah Boomah Boomah and he launches one and we all C It Go…. It was not the game but it has been the time we have spent with all of those who love the Sox in our families….

For my dad, Bill Crooks Jr., who has followed the Sox for 55 years and is still here for me to call and remember those nights at the park.

For his dad who is not, and all people who spent time with us as kids taking us to games and rooting for the Sox.

For my children, Will and Brittany, who now are the 4th generation of Sox fans in the Crooks family.

For my mom, Pennie Crooks, who never missed a game with me on the TV. A true lifelong fan.

For my uncle, Don Joyce, win it for his friend Johnny P.

For my uncle, Gene, who sent me a pack of baseball cards every week.

**—Bill Crooks III
(BuckybleepinLittle)**

Win it for my mom; she's responsible for me being the diehard Sox fan I am today. When I got my Sox tattoo, she, instead of flipping out like a typical parent, said, "I want one!"

When the Sox were down 0-2 to Oakland, she decided the Red Sox needed some more luck, so what did she do? She nailed—not tacked, NAILED—her authentic 1967 Pennant to the wall. We remember how that series turned out. This year, down 0-3 to the Yanks (after bawling mid-game 3), I decided they needed more luck again, so I pinned a "We Still Believe" button on the 1967 Pennant. I was in Cask when they won the ALCS and called home amidst all the screaming in the bar so that my mom and I could have a quick cry together. Win it for her, for training the next generation of diehards.

Win it for my sister, who's an officer in the Army and stuck about 2 hours away from St. Louis right now, rooting hard for the Red Sox amidst loads of Cards and Yanks fans (nobody ever said the Army attracts the most intelligent of people).

What the heck, win it for me, because when I went to the park to get my 10th Man Plan on that cold December morning, after taking batting practice I snuck out to the bleachers to check out my seat. Nobody was around, so I laid down in a patch of snow on the stairs, and made a snow angel. So, now the Sox have their very own angel in the outfield watching over them.

Win it because, one day, I want my kids to learn a new chant: "year 2000," the last year that the Yankees won the World Series.

—Yvette d'Entremont

Win it for my brother-in-law, who used to work the scoreboard at Fenway and has begged his whole life for the Sox to win. He once said, "Trot Nixon is the only player I know who can hit a two run homer with the bases empty."

For some reason that makes sense to me.

—John G. Comas

Win it for ....

Amen. I add my grandfather Pasquale—I want this one for him.

Watching the World Series with him and seeing his pride as every member of the extended family called to offer congratulations was the best gift I could ask for.

—Guido Zarrella

Win it for my dad and his five siblings, who grew up diehard Sox fans but were so hurt by 1986 that believing became so very hard. Their belief is there, deep inside, but more than belief, give them back their faith.

For my Nana and Grampy, who have repressed the Sox even more so than their children.

For my mom, who screamed so loud at Aaron Boone. And for her brother, who always expects the worst to happen.

For my Grampa who was at Teddy Ballgame's last game and turned 80 on October 24, 2004—the day of Game 1. Grampa stays up and watches every game and he walks around proudly wearing his new ALCS Championship shirt. He has been waiting so long. The longest wait of which I personally know.

For my Gramma, who stays up and watches the games with Grampa (yes even the late ones), even if she doesn't quite "get" the game.

Win it for my brother and sister, who collectively flipped out after Game 7 2003 and like the best Sox fans, live and die with every pitch. (There is at least one hole in the walls of our house because of them.)

For my friends, around the country and abroad, who can't be in Boston, their true or adopted home, during this wonderful time.

For Red Sox Nation, because of the pain we have endured, during my time on Earth and before that. So we can watch Buckner highlights and not cringe; so we can finally have a definite answer to the (media-propagated) "curse."

And, selfishly, for me, who has taken leave from volunteering with Habitat for Humanity International in the Deep South. Who has traveled over a thousand miles from Americus, Georgia, back to Massachusetts just so I could be in Boston while the Sox played the Series. My decision boggled the mind of more than one person (and depleted my bank account), but makes complete sense to me.

Win it for the unborn future generations of Red Sox Nation, so they may never experience our pain.

—David DiGiammarino

Win it for ....

Wonderful thread! Thanks. Allow me to add my parents, Roy and Rose Smith, and dear family friend Jack, who are, with many others, pulling strings from the beyond to make this happen.

—Catherine Doucette

Win it for ....

My family is all from Boston, so there was never any doubt where my allegience would be. My dad is more of a rabid Celts fan, and he's in Italy right now, hopefully tossing back more than a few Chiantis with my mom, aunt and uncle (from Peabody) in celebration.

I think this one goes out to my Gramps, Tony Blase. I can remember as a kid sitting in his small kitchen off White Street in East Boston, him drinking coffee with anisette, talking about the Sox while my grandmother toasted some fresh Italian bread for breakfast. I can recall weeks in the summer spent on Bayside Road in East

Falmouth at the little cottage he and my grandmother bought in 1963 after my mom, his only child, got married. I can remember me and my three brothers sleeping on the crowded floor of this small two-bedroom cottage. I can remember sitting down to lunch on a Saturday afternoon, the radio on, my Gramps pounding Red White and Blues or Falstaffs as we listened to the Sox. I can remember my first sip of beer coming from his cup, and I still haven't gotten over an affinity for cheap brewskis. And I can remember how those times solidified my love for the Sox, and how for my eighth birthday, I asked for and received a Sox jacket with my name embroidered on it as a result of that love.

This one was for Anthony Blase, my Papa. Born a couple of years prior to the last Sox WS victory, died October of 1993. He was one of the funniest, kindest and most loving people I've ever been lucky enough to know. I'd love to be with him to see his reaction, but his smile and laugh are imprinted on my brain, so I have a pretty good idea of what it was.

—D. Beerabelli

Win it for everyone who grew up secretly listening to the Red Sox on the radio (WTIC in my case) after their parents had sent them to bed. Win it for all the current and former players already mentioned and all the members of Red Sox Nation—past and present.

This is an historic moment. I absolutely believe the Red Sox will win. But, no matter what, Red Sox fans are the greatest sports fans in the world. We are a family. We pass our love for the Sox on from generation to generation and, no matter what, we stand by our team and each other.

Thank you for this amazing thread. Thank you to everyone out there reading it. And thank you to the Red Sox players and the organization for giving us the opportunity to feel the way we do right now.

—Karl Leonard

Win it for One Nation Under Guapo, our defunct fantasy baseball league.

—David Palmer

Win it for ....

Win one for my grandfather who was born in 1906 and went to the final game of the World Series in 1918. He spent the rest of his life waiting for the next one. I would see him every Sunday growing up and we will always talk about the Red Sox. As he got older and his memory grew worse, he would still remember his team. He would always ask me how his boys were doing and if I thought this year would be the year. He passed away a couple of years ago, with his dream never fulfilled. Papa—this is the year. Your boys are going to do it. And we'll all be thinking about you when it happens.

—Mike

Win it for my Aunt Neenee (Eileen) and my Uncle Dick, who watched my brother and me while my parents worked from the time we were 2 until we were about 5.

My aunt is one of the most amazing women I know, having battled breast cancer and the tumors spreading to her brain for the better part of 10 years. She battled hard to make it to her son's wedding this summer, before having to head back to the hospital for treatment.

My uncle, a dedicated man, has battled his own health problems (a series of heart attacks), which caused him to have to retire from his job as a police office. He's a true old school Sox fan, rooting for the laundry and not the players.

This morning I got the early morning call, the call that everyone dreads, that my aunt has been moved home to be with family over her last few days.

It would be completely unfair for this cruel, unfeeling, spiteful disease to take her from this world before the Sox finish this out.

So don't delay. Win this in 4 games. Consciously, I don't think my aunt will even know—the tumor and treatments have taken their toll. Subconciously, she'll know—every Sox fan will.

Please give my aunt and uncle, two of the nicest people in the world, a little happiness over the next couple of days.

For what it's worth, my aunt made it through the series, passing away the day after Thanksgiving.

**—Ryan Toohil
(Randy Kutchers Mullet)**

Win it for....

I wanted to add a whole list of people, my father, grandfather (who is hanging on for this exact reason), my brothers, my wife, grandmother (who never got the chance), but mostly I wanted to say win it for everyone reading through this thread, welling up in their offices, dorm rooms, or living rooms, showing how a game played by 9 grown men, can somehow bring out the rawest of emotions and bring even more grown men to tears.

Red Sox fans don't band together because of a C***e, or a losing streak of too many years, its because it connects us to our families, our friends, the loved ones in our lives. It's the comforting smell of your grandparents house from when you were a child, a spirit that makes us recall the wonderful (and sometimes not so wonderful) moments and people of our entire lives. The Red Sox are not just 9 athletes on a patch of grass, they are the millions of lives who have been pushing for this one moment for 4 generations.

—Brian Blackwell

Win it for my late grandfather and my father who have endured far more than my 23 years of suffering and maudlin enjoyment. I have learned more from being a Red Sox fan than from any other facet of my life…. I am forever grateful for the opportunity to love the greatest sport and team in history. In the end, baseball is not life or death and contrary to the old adage, the Red Sox are not life or death…. Life is that indescribable foreknowledge that even in death, our "misery" would someday be eased by our beloved Red Sox. Someday is now and the pain of many years of suffering is resting easy next to my late grandfather. This one is for you!

—Ghost of Ted Williams

Win it for my dad, who passed away on 10/20/93. When I was a seven-year-old boy, he introduced me to and shared the Impossible Dream, which was where my love for this awesome team all began. Last night, I watched the Sox greatest victory (so far, this year) with his 8-year-old grandson, Jeremiah, who in turn is catching the fever. We talked about my dad and all he taught me about the game. Mom called after the game, and we shared tears of joy, and a tear of grief.

**—Bob Snee
(OregonSoxFan)**

Win it for....

I moved to this country to be with a Red Sox fan. He broke my heart, but instilled in me an unshakable love of the Sox. My mother and sister demanded my return home in the wake of my crushing broken relationship. They are still waiting; I could never go home the Year The Sox Did It. And so long as the Sox still play, I never will. So please, win it for my lonely mother, who ends every phone call with "Go Sox!" though she wouldn't know a baseball if it hit her square between the eyes. And for my sister, who in an effort to preserve our closeness now follows Sox games on the internet (often starting at 2 a.m.) so that she can discuss the game with me the following day. They will never understand my obsession with the Sox, but they never questioned my decision to stay here for them.

**—Allison Gibney
(DaDamoness)**

Win it for all the ushers and longtime Fenway employees that have put so much time and heart into working for their beloved team.

Win it for Joe B. and every other season ticket holder.

Finally, win it for my brother Jon, who has been there with me every game.

—Joe Dorant

Win it for my late brother David, the biggest Red Sox fan I ever knew. He would be so damn proud of this team.

—Kiss My Aase

Win it for ....

I'm a Giants fan, but I've been mesmerized by reading the "win it for…." thread. I want the Sox to win it for all you faithful RSN people because of your passion and depth of suffering.

And besides, if the Sox can break their curse, that gives Giants fans the hope that our SF curse may someday be lifted too (hopefully in my lifetime)!

—Missy and Boo

Win it for every little kid in the Fenway stands, peeking meekly through their fingers at every tense moment.

Win it so they can grow up unencumbered, always confident in this team.

**—Mike
(Let it Flo)**

Win it for ....

My husband and I are 2nd generation SF Giant fans. Our 22-year-old daughter has never watched baseball on television, not interested. That all changed with Game 4 of the ALCS. Since that night she has watched every game, every inning, and every out.

Win it for all the new fans your team has created and hopefully they will become as passionate about the game as RSN.

—SLOGiant

Win it for my grandmother, Carolyn Salsbury. Due to family differences that I will never fully understand, I was not able to meet her for the first time until this summer (I am 27 years old). It turns out she has looked forward to meeting me as much as I was meeting her. It's hard to explain, but my grandparents were never mentioned growing up because of the family problems. I learned about her when she was announced as a winner of a Sox trip to spring training in the late 1980s. I barely knew I had a grandmother, let alone that she was a Sox fan like me. It was so great to meet her and have her as a part of my life. I never met my grandfather (he passed away five years ago), but was shown that their shared gravestone has a Red Sox logo on it over her name. She says she wants to see them win one before she passes away.

On the Sunday after the Angels series my grandmother had a heart attack. She's been on a respirator ever since.

It's been a roller-coaster ride. Some days it looks like she won't make it. She's still on a respirator and it is touch and go. She's barely conscious of the environment around her. She's been fighting for the past two weeks just like her beloved Red Sox. We're pretty sure she knows what is going on. The nurses put the game on every night for her. I pray multiple times every day that she makes it. She deserves to see them win.

—Joe Salsbury

Win it for Don and Walt Norton. Don and Walt lived and breathed the Red Sox until they passed away in their mid-20s. Although muscular dystrophy took their ability to play ball, it never took their passion for the Red Sox.

We spent countless nights together watching the Sox, including lots of crying in '75, '78 and '86.

This time, let the blessed group of 25 win the WS for Don and Walt.

—Mark Mierzejewski

Win it for the love of my life, my wife:

• born between Games 2 and 3 of the 1967 World Series (coincidence that it was an off day? I think not)

• who came home from grade school to watch and be heartbroken in 1978

• who died a little at college (with a lot of MFY and MFM fans) in 1986

• who took me on our first date to Fenway Park in 1993, where she captured my heart by knowing the answer to the trivia question, jumping up and down and yelling, "Bernie Carbo! Bernie Carbo!" (that day's attendance quiz: "If you guessed, 'I'm going to marry this girl— YOU'RE RIGHT'")

• who has converted me (lifelong Phillies fan) since we moved back here in 1999 to experience five of the best years of baseball, in the best baseball town, anywhere

• who died a little more with me in 2003, telling me during Game 7 against the MFY, "My grandparents hated the Yankees, my parents hated the Yankees, I hate the Yankees, and by God, someday when we have children, THEY will hate the Yankees!"

• who has convinced me to take a road trip to enemy territory each summer (taking over the Ted in Atlanta this July)

• who took me to one game this year (Grandma's seats), on July 24—four rows from where Tek woke them up, and Billy Mueller helped start to turn it around vs Fruitbat

• whose father, a devoted fan since the days of Pesky, Doerr, and Williams, woke her up during Game 6 in 1975 because something truly special was happening and he didn't want her to miss it

• whose grandmother, this incredible Sicilian matriarch, still catches every game at age 92 and anticipates spring training with her daughter Rita (yes, the patron saint of impossible dreams) like a little kid

Win it for the people in RSN through whose lives the fabric of the Sox runs; those for whom hope springs eternal.

If that isn't enough, win it for yourselves. Win it for each other.

GO SOX!

—Michael F. Gilronan

Win it for all the Sox fans living in Yankeeland....

—Nick Steenstra

Win it for my son Dylan. He was only 6 years old in '99, and in retrospect, he was a sharp kid. He saw all the balls and calls bounce the Yankees way. After the ALCS he asked a great question, "Dad, wouldn't be easier to switch teams?" Trying to be the prophetic, wise father, I said, "Easier isn't better. This is going to be better, and when the time comes, we will enjoy it 1000 times more." May we enjoy it tonight.

Win it for my wife Tina. After game 3 of this year's ALCS she told me that she felt bad for me. She was hoping beyond hope that this would have been the year, that we could finally put this all behind us. I told her not to feel bad for me, that I was enjoying the ride, and that we had to find a way to win game 4. She enjoyed last week's baseball in a way she never has. We have walked around nodding our heads "Yes" since the end of game 4, and it has been fun.

Win it for my daughter Alycia. She doesn't understand strategy, but she loves to go to a game. She roots hard for our team. Win or lose, she's behind them all the way. And she loves the snacks at the ballpark.

Win it for my 86-year-old grandmother. The old-fashioned New England persistence that I learned from her has carried me a long way. May it carry us to one more win.

Win it.

—George Woodbury
(Visalia Oak)

Win it for ....

My grandfather and "Sito" who are long gone now but have been sitting next to me in spirit the entire way.

My mother (the single mom) who brought me to my first Sox game (age 7) and allowed me to stay up waaaay past bedtime when the Sox were on West Coast trips.

All my friends who have come close to giving up but NEVER did.

Finally, to the big-grinned 80-year-old man who was behind me in WalMart today and talked about waiting his entire life for a World Series. His just-as-old wife looking at him with tears in her eyes, knowing the moment he's waited for is upon us....

Good times.

**—Jeramie Whipple
(SoxinMaine)**

Win it for my brother Jay. He is a huge fan who taught me everything I know about baseball and opened up my eyes to all that is the Red Sox. He'll never know how much I love him.

Win it for all my friends in NYC who have been there for me over the years and helped me through a very rough personal time.

Win it for my mother. She was taken in a car accident on October 31st, 1988. The joy this would bring to her children would make her smile from above. Love and miss you every day.

—James "Buddy" Villani

Win it for my grandfather, born right after the Sox won in 1918, and then passed away a week after the loss in '86, devastated and heartbroken at the Sox loss.

Win it so I can go down with a Guinness, and drink one with him at the gravesite. Win so I can cry tears I've never cried.

Win it for Red Sox fans who are soldiers overseas who need something to hold onto.

Win it for Red Sox Nation, the hurt will go away. The pain stops. Tonight the heavens open, and it is good.

Love you and miss you Gramps, this one's for you. And all of the rest of the family of this board watching with ya tonight.

(a few days later)

I did go down to the grave today and had a beer with Gramps, and shed a few tears. And then felt very very warm and smiled, almost like a hug from above. Sunlight for the few minutes I was there before going back to an overcast day. Something special I tell ya, something very special.

Something special here boys and girls, something VERY special. Thank you.

(11:16 P.M. after game 4)

Hey Gramps…. I'll see you tommorow. With another Guinness. It'll be sweet. It finally happened.

—Dave R.

Win it for my mother, fighting a battle with breast cancer. She had a dose of chemo the morning of game seven, was very drowsy and sick. Nothing could have brought a smile to her face more than the Red Sox winning the AL pennant, dancing on the field at Yankee Stadium. She might not make it to next year's World Series, this might be her last chance. Win it and win immortality in Boston. For her, for the nation, for yourselves.

—Anonymous

Win it for my brother, Eric Vander May, 1971-2004, who was and always will be a faithful RS fan and the tenth man for the Sox at Fenway Park. You beat me to season tickets buddy!

Believe the RS can do this! Believe the souls of RS Nation are always with us!

—Matt VanderMay

Win it for....

For Dad, 83, and Mom, 79, and anyone else who is running out of chances to see this happen.

For every player who walked out of Yankee Stadium heartbroken on 10/17/03 and who wasn't there for the redemption. Nomar, Todd Walker, Damian Jackson, Adrian Brown, John Burkett, Scott Sauerbeck and anyone else I may have forgotten. Even Jeff Suppan.

Red Sox players, win it for yourselves. When the '75 and '78 editions lost, I was disappointed, but they were so talented I was sure they would get back. By 1986, only Dewey, Jim Rice and Bob Stanley remained from the '78 team, and I had matured enough baseball-wise to realize that '86 was their chance, and they didn't get it done. This might be the only chance most of the '04 team gets. Don't waste it.

Thanks.

**—John P. Duncliffe
(soxfaninyankeeland)**

Win it for Ann, the lady who sits across the aisle from me, in Section 40, who has been in the same seats for about 40 years. She comes to EVERY game, holding the radio to her ear and scoring every play.

Win it for the next generation of Red Sox Nation.

Let our kids learn the value of setting a goal, working hard and concentrating on reaching that goal. Remind them that even the best have to practice and learn every day.

Let our kids learn that "no one bats 1.000." Let them learn that if you fail, it doesn't mean you quit, or blame somebody else. Let them learn that failure and hardship happen, and their response to those situations will define them, positively or negatively.

—Jeff Bray

Win it for ....

Great thread! I'll throw in a win it for my late great mother-in-law, Irene, or as it reads on her headstone, Irene, the Red Sox Queen. Irene actually had a sports radio show out of Worcester over 20 years ago, the first woman radio sports show host that I know of. There never was or will be a greater and more loyal Red Sox fan!

My beloved and now deceased grandfather, from whom I inherited my undying passion for this team. I have many great memories of him, not the least of which was the sound of Red Sox play-by-play coming from his room on his old beat-up transistor radio. And of his yelling at the radio when the Sox made an error, and of his laughing when the good guys pulled out another come from behind win. The Sox were his love, his passion, and I'm sure, his shelter from the storm, just as they've been and still are for many elderly and infirmed. I worshipped him, except for the one thing he had I didn't—he'd lived through a Red Sox championship. This year, GrampaPutt, this year!

—Dana Crawford

Win it for my dad, my brother and me. My dad and brother became fans when they moved to Boston in '73.... I did when I was born there in '75. We realize baseball is just a sport and the Sox are just a team, but nevertheless it brings us closer together and that is one of the main reasons why I (we) love the Sox. They are more than sport, they are love, hate, sorrow, joy, excitement, frustration and every other emotion they elicit among family and friends. They are more than sport; they are relationships. That's why we love them and that's why we want them to win. To share this moment with those we love. I don't think many people outside of RSN understand this.... but those within RSN do. I am confident of this.

Go Sox! Win it for us.

—Noah Salvione

Win it for my dad, Robert F. Elliott. He's taught me everything he knows about the game. He would play catch with me for hours when I was little, always told me to hold the ball because "We weren't playing 'drop.'" Now every once in a while we throw around for about ten minutes and his arm gets tired. So many bad things have happened to him in his life, I just want him to have something good to think about besides me and my sister. He has the original Impossible Dream record sitting on top of his television as I'm writing this. He may not have gone to hundreds of games at Fenway, especially lately, but he loves the Sox more than he shows. This one's for you, Dad.

—Mike Elliott
Derry, NH

Win it for my dad, who took me to my first Sox game when I was just a six-year-old girl who didn't care about baseball at all and who made him miss the better part of the game with a bunch of trips to get me popcorn, ice cream and soda and to take me to the bathroom. He still tells the story of the 3 run homer by Jim Rice that we missed while he took me down to the bathroom in the left field grandstand. Win it for him because despite that disastrous first trip to see the Sox, he didn't give up on my becoming a member of Red Sox Nation and took me again at 12, when I was a much better game companion. Win it for him because in game after game he taught me how to keep score and made sure that I would never be just a casual, fairweather fan. At those games we went to, he told me stories of buying bleacher seats with his friends and then sneaking under the gate that used to divide the bleachers from the grandstand to get better seats. Win it for him because of the way he held my hand tighter and kept me closer to him the day he took me to my first Sox/Yankees game and told me "Karen, it's going to be a little different today," as we walked by a fight happening outside Who's on First. Win it for all the opening day tickets he somehow managed to get when he would skip work and I would skip school and we would sit at Fenway and freeze with a big smile on our faces in April.

Win it for all the newspaper articles about the Sox he clipped and highlighted and rolled up and sent to me while I was 300 miles away at college. Win it for the Red Sox hats he bought and sent to my best friends at college —upstate New Yorkers who joined me in my hatred for the Yankees even if they weren't huge baseball fans. Win it for the enormous banner he brought to the parade they had even though they didn't win it all in 1986, for the picture of him in the Metro that appeared the day after the first baseball games were played after September 11th—my dad in his full Red Sox gear showing his patriotism and love of the Sox at the same time. Win it for the ridiculous amount of letters he has sent to players, ownership and anyone else affiliated with the Sox since he first became a fan in 1957. Win it for him because he still can't watch any clips of the 1986 series ("I'll never forget the look on Boggsy's face in the dugout after that game was over, Karen") and because he still yells at Grady Little when he sees clips of the 8th inning of Game 7 last year as though it is happening all over again. Win it for him because he gets giddy on his birthday every year like a little kid because his birthday is the same as his favorite player, Yaz. Win it because he loves the new Ted Williams statue at Gate B and makes sure to touch his shoe after every game he goes to. Win it for him because his radio ID at work is "1918" and he has suffered 28 years of non-Sox fans at work taping clips of all the Sox foibles to his locker there and writing "losers" inside the brim of his ragged old Sox hat.

Win it for my dad because he still has no voice today after yelling like a madman during Games 4 and 5 at Fenway Park. Win it for him because after work today he headed over to Yawkey Way and bought me a "World Series 2004" hat with that Red Sox "B" on it. Win it because I never again want him to turn to me like he did last year after the ALCS and say, "Karen, I am sorry I made you a Red Sox fan." Just win it!!

—Karen Costello

Win it for my grandmother who passed away three years ago. Some of my earliest Sox memories are of watching games at her house. Nonna would clap her hands with delight when they won, but could turn ferocious if the Sox blew it.

Win it for my parents, brothers and uncles. Many of our family gatherings have centered around important Sox games. We've shared some joy but a lot more misery over the years.

And this is selfish, but win it for my adolescent self. In April 1986 I decided to truly follow this team. I was 11 years old. Roger Clemens was my first crush. I cut out *Globe* articles and plastered posters on my walls. I looked through my Red Sox scrapbook every day. On a perfect September afternoon, I attended my first game. Oil Can Boyd pitched and I almost got Calvin Schiraldi's autograph, but was too shy to break through the crowd. A month later this shy, awkward girl proudly told the popular kids on the bus that the Sox were going to win the World Series. This was in western Mass., where New York fans have infiltrated, and they all laughed and said there was no way the Sox would win. That Monday I pretended I was sick so I wouldn't have to face the ridicule. Like so much of my adolescence, my heart had been broken.

Win it for those of us who have trouble believing that good things can happen, and that hopes aren't always dashed, if you only have faith.

Thanks.

—Deb Whittemore
Windsor, CT

Win it for my father, who cried in 1946, and 1986, and didn't get the chance to see this team, one I know he would love. And win it for his younger brother, who if only by phone I get to share this with, for which I am very grateful.

—Jim Stoker

Win it for ....

It's time for me to add my father, who gave me his name, to this list. He served his family, his country (AAF, WWII) and his community with distinction, but that's a story for another day. He was a great fan of baseball in general, and the Red Sox in particular. He and my mother told me great stories about sitting on the porch listening to the crack of the bat over the sounds of the crickets in the hot Southern summer night as the mill league teams played just down the street. The mill town he came from happened to be the home of Billy Goodman, which cemented his Sox fan status, although my grandfather had also been a Sox fan; even back then the Sox were the alternative to the grandiose Yankees. One of the great experiences for my dad was when he and my mother were in Washington for a Sox-Senators game and Goodman called my dad over to meet Ted Williams. Contrary to stereotype, Ted was totally gracious and spent a number of minutes in conversation. As with many of you, I could write a long time about my father, baseball and myself, but I'll just say he passed on Sox craziness to me, and it's "in my blood like holy wine, so bitter and so sweet." I was living in Somerville in 1978 and when I told my father how the Sox had broken my heart and brain, he said you just needed to know that baseball could do that, and proceeded to tell me some old stories. My dad moved on over a decade ago without seeing the Sox reach the promised land. I believe that once you cross over to the undiscovered country you don't look back, so I don't have a sense that he's watching the idiots. Instead, he is with me in blood and loving memory. The more time passes, the more you realize how powerful that is. Thanks, Dad, for everything, including my connection to this great game and this great team.

—William Robertson

Win it for my mom Christiane (died April 6th, 2002). She didn't know anything about baseball or the Red Sox but she made it possible for me to make a language trip to Boston in the year 2000 where I fell in love with the game of baseball and esspecially with the Boston Red Sox.

This team really helped me (I'm 20 years old now) overcome her death and brought so much joy to me !

I love this team!!!

—Clemens Schlipp
(Pedro1984)

Win it for ....

On October 4th, early in the morning, with her loving family beside her, my mother died. She was a lifelong Red Sox fan. Born in Bar Harbor, the daughter of a farmer and the grand-daughter of a sea captain, she attended college at Wheelock and graduated in 1939. While at school in Boston her love of the Red Sox grew. In the fifties it solidified through watching her two young sons play the game with an absolute joy. Until her death she listened to or watched every game her Red Sox played.

What tragedy. She lived for eighty-six years and not one of those days were the Red Sox a World Champion. She was born in December of 1918. I believe it is her fate and her goodwill to us that her life bookended our Championships.

Boston Red Sox, win this one for my mom who will be watching form the most comfortable and best seat in the house.

—The Fleischner and Morneau families

Win it for my late grandfather, Mitchell Creeger. He pulled me into RSN almost 2 decades ago, sitting in his den with him on visits to Longmeadow MA, where he watched every televised game and never gave up hope.

Win it for my 1-year-and-2-month-old son, Dylan Mitchell. He may not be able to remember this year himself, but I would never let him forget it. And no matter what the future held, he would never have to hear that they never won it in his lifetime.

Win it for my father, James, and brother, Aaron. My attempts to convert them to members of RSN are beginning to work.

—Seth Bates

Win it for everyone knows what it's like to sit on the porch alone in the summer twilight listening to the game, without a care in the world, except that someday, maybe someday....

**—Scott Reoch
(Who the Hell is Stan Papi)**

Win it for everyone who has seen a Red Sox World Series without seeing a win. Fans for that long, they surely deserve it.

But also win it for everyone who is seeing a Sox Series for the first time, or who were too young to remember the '86 one.

Win it for the college kids far from Boston, huddled in their dorm rooms in front of the TV, sharing secret smiles with other kids they see around campus wearing Sox hats, missing late classes to watch the games, hunched over laptops showing the Gameday screen in coffee shops and lecture halls all across the country.

Win it for the younger kids who have a chance to have their first Sox memories be happy ones.

Win it for the parents of these kids, who were brave enough to raise them as Sox fans and now have a chance to be rewarded for their emotional gamble.

Just.... win.

**—Samara Pearlstein
(Boston Fan in Michigan)**

Win it for ....

I can't post because I'm not a member, so maybe you can add Ellis to the list. He's been my favorite player since he came up and when he came back to the Red Sox last winter I told everyone I knew the stars had finally aligned. Win it for Ellis Burks.

**—Susannah Gallus
(ellisrena)**

Win it for ....

For my father, William (1922-1989), who brought me to the hallowed grounds of Fenway for the first time in 1967 and taught me the proper way to sit in the Holy See of Baseball, to revere its images and pay tribute to its acolytes past, present and future.

For my daughter, Kirstin, who was 3 months old in October 1986 and lay huddled in my arms through each of those 7 games, and who is now ready to take on the awesome responsibility as a torchbearer for the next generation of The Nation.

Most of all win it for the Game itself. Baseball needs this team as much as this team needs baseball. Secure the sport for all time with a story that will be told on grandparents knees far and wide, extolling the virtues of the best that resides within all of us.

—67dreamin

Win it for Homer William George Jr., a great man who despite his inability to pronounce the names of the players correctly was a true diehard. A man who raised his son to be loyal and whose friendship has been just that. If we do it, I'll be thinking of you Homer.

—Darren Chisnell

Win it for ....

May you all, if not tonight, then within the next few days, taste and enjoy the glory of a Red Sox World Championship. To forever erase the 1918 chants and to send the Senior Circuit down the tubes with another October setback.

Win it for all relatives of Sox fans who are no longer living, and for the parents who have raised another generation of the Nation. And for the children, nephews and nieces who will carry the flag in decades to come and relate tales of 2004 when all was right in the hardball universe.

Win it for my friend, Mark Twomey, who now lives in Pennsylvania but who has suffered and followed the Sox from Mass. to NY to PA since 1967. We took in several "Chi-Bo Classics" at Fenway during our college years from 1978-82. And it was me who convinced him not to stand in line for playoff tickets in 1978 after watching the Sox beat Toronto on the second-to-last day of the season, telling him there was no way the Yanks would lose to Cleveland on the last day of the season. Perhaps it was best he didn't witness the Monday game anyway.

Win it for Bernie Corbett and Ed Carpenter, both long-time Sox fans and diehard BU guys.

Win it for all who hope to see the day when the bubble doesn't burst and the trap door stays shut.

Win it for Dalton Jones and Bernie Carbo and Dave Stapleton.

And win it so that once the 1918 Curse is vanquished; we can start working on that 1917 Curse that the "other" Sox are carrying around.

Carpe Diem.

—Mark in White Plains

Win it for ....

Last year I posted a diatribe in P&G after He Who Shall Not Be Named left in Pedro in Game 7. I almost gave up just thinking of how close we were. In particular, I was thinking of my grandfather who instilled in me the love I have for the Red Sox.

Pepe was a great guy. He had an 8th grade education because he had to leave school to work on his family farm, but he was one of the smartest men I ever knew. He fought in WW2, spending 2 and a half years in

Europe fighting the Germans then came home and raised 3 daughters. He worked on boilers his whole life, and while he never made a lot of money, he always gave his family everything they needed. He could fix everything himself and my earliest memories are of standing next to him in his garage while he worked on something and listening to the Sox on the radio with him. Fortunately, because I spent time with him listening to the Sox, I learned a whole new world of swearing, too.

I have a lot of memories of him and most involve the Sox. So when they win this thing I'm getting in my truck, driving to Burrillville, RI, and I'm going to sit next to him, and he and I will have a beer to celebrate. Just like it should be.

Just win.

—Mr. Weebles

Win it for Paul Garber.

1918—Boston Red Sox win World Series.

1919—Paul Garber is born.

May 2004—Paul Garber, lifelong Red Sox fan, dies at the ripe old age of 85, never having seen the Red Sox win the World Series.

October 2004—Red Sox will win the World Series!

Grandpa, I only wish you were able to be a part of just one more BoSox season. Love you always.

—Hugh Garber

Win it for ....

When it comes down to it, the Red Sox are just a sports team, and baseball is just a game. People who are not on a Sox high probably would not admit that they'd rather win the WS than have their favorite candidate win the election, or that they'd rather break up with a loved one than see them lose it this time.

Probably they don't mean it, really. But here's the thing: there is something about the Red Sox that has attached them enough to make them say these things, however much in jest. This is not just a clean-cut team, a factory-processed bunch of machines: the Red Sox have become friends to us, they have become family members. It's not just the .301 averages or the high OBP numbers: it's the weird hair, the tears in their eyes on Wednesday, the personalities, the trust, the…. intangibles.

There, I've said it. It's not the "intangibles" that make the Sox a good baseball team, but it's the intangibles that have made us love them through the years. If David Ortiz was affected by a message of faith, then it's not so silly to imagine the fans being captured by the same.

So win it for a beloved elderly neighbor who is 97 and has not seen the Sox win since she was ten. For my friend

Helen from CA who admitted that this team is growing on her. For my nephew Dominick, age 7, who has gone from thinking abstractly of me as an aunt to bonding with me over his first two live Sox games.

But most of all, win it for the very fact that this team does mean something more than averages and wins to its fans—call it the intangibles or call it faith or call it love: it has given us a reason to believe in something that has no practical effects on our lives but means something JUST BECAUSE. Win it for the very institution of faith.

—Diana M. Gauvin

Win it for my 10-year-old son Charlie who fell asleep listening to Game 7 of the 2003 ALCS assuming the Sox would win. When he awakened the next morning, he asked me, eagerly, "Did we win, Dad?" When I told him, gently, "No, we did not win," his anguished moan startled me. I knew I had raised him as a Red Sox fan and I began to question whether that was a good thing.

—Michael Beers
Newton, Massachusetts

Win it for ....

Some of you will understand and remember. Some of you won't but you will get the idea, years of heartbreak and loss. This is a shot at redemption and a time to remember all those who watched, listened, played and loved the game. A time to remember all those we hold dear to our hearts past and present.

I say this, to all of you who made fun of me and my love of the Sox. To all of you who think it's just a game, ask the millions around the world if it's just a game? To those of you who doubted the Sox could bring us this far—I never relinquished my belief or hope, even after the devastating loss to the Yankees on Saturday by the score of 19-8. This put the Sox in a 0-3 hole to the Yankees. We stood on the precipice of elimination. It was a valley for sure, but without valleys how do you experience the joy of climbing to the top of the mountain? We reached the top of the mountain Wednesday night as the Sox crushed our arch enemy. The Evil Empire, finally defeated by a Red Sox team in the postseason. I cried. I laughed. It was pure joy. I want to experience that feeling again when we conquer another mountain, winning the World Series, to know the joy of accomplishment and the reward for believing in the Sox for so many years.

The Drama, the intensity, history in the making, two great foes squaring off as if it were the OK Corral. Staring one another down until the first shot is fired. The setting: Tombstone, AZ. Tonight, it's Fenway Park, game one of the World Series. Let that first shot be fired by the Red Sox blasting a home run into the heart of the Red Birds. Let the last game be a Red Sox victory....

Baseball is a kid's game but we all have that little kid inside of us and we never forget the first time we listened to a game on a transistor radio, watched a game on TV in black and white, and played our first Little League game or the first time going to the shrine known as Fenway Park. Watching the Red Sox reminds me of that childhood innocence. It's still there, small as it may be now.

I was introduced to Fenway Park, the "Field of Dreams" in April of 1967 by my dad. We always listened to games on the radio or watched them on TV but I had never been to Fenway Park. I remember walking up the tunnel towards the field and seeing the outfield grass for the first time. I had never seen anything so green. It looked as if someone had manicured emeralds, I thought, "This must be what Ireland looks like," from all the talks I had with my grandmother as she told me about the old country and how green it was over there. I will never forget that first trip to Fenway and I will never forget my dad for bringing me to Fenway. My "Field of Dreams" were vacant lots and cement sidewalks growing up in Dorchester. Vacant lots for wiffleball and stickball in the streets is where we passed hours and hours of summer days and nights emulating our heroes, Fisk, Lynn and Rice. I was in awe of Fenway. It was larger than life. The lights shining down onto the field made it seem brighter than day. Then the wall, The Green Monster. It wasn't as imposing on TV as Yaz patrolled left field. There it was, larger than I imagined it would look like. It was brutally cold that night but did I care? We took a cab home, Dad, Steve and me. I can still remember Dad talking to the cab driver about Dick Williams; they thought he could do something for the Sox that year. Oh my! Something magical happened that year. It was the year known as the "Impossible Dream" how can one forget?

Everywhere you went you heard Sinatra singing, "To dream, the impossible dream...."

I was just a kid in 1967 the memory of the loss to the Cardinals is there but it's not as clear as the collapse of 1974 or the World Series of 1975, the one game elimination with the Yankees in 1978 or the heartbreaking loss five outs away from winning the 1986 World Series. Forever, they will be etched into my memory. I now know how my dad must have felt in 1946 with Enos Slaughter running round the bases to break a 3-3 tie or 1967 when a steam train known as Bob Gibson ripped the heart out of my dad's chest. We came so close, only to have all dreams of a World Series title dashed. This is the year to vanquish all of those memories.

Witnessing the blood on Schilling's sock speaks to the human spirit. He was wasted after 4 innings but he kept on until the 7th. It is truly the human spirit that gives me reason to believe, for that, I give my reasons as to why I want the Sox to win it all. For the human spirit of those no longer with us and for those of us lucky enough to still be here and have stood by the Sox all these years. I say Win it for:

Win it for my Nana as she loved the Sox as much as she loved talking about Ireland. I miss talking about both subjects with her. Win it for her and the old country.

Win it for all my nieces and nephews, the next generation of Sox fans. Win it for my brothers and sisters: Steve, Laurie and Lisa and their families. Win it for all of my cousins. Win it for Aunt Theresa. Win it for Uncle

Leo, another lifelong Sox fan. Uncle Leo thanks for all the memories you gave me. "You can take the kid out of the city but you can't take the city out of the kid." Win it for Uncle Johnny, a true sportsman of boxing and football. A great Red Sox fan taken far too early…. Win it for all of them.

Win it for Christine, a very special young lady to me. The glove I gave her is my way of passing the torch to feel the passion and the bond handed down from one generation to the next generation of Sox fans. This is how the transfer for the love of the game begins and the love of the Sox is forever engraved into her heart. Win it for her.

Win it for another special person in my heart, Jane. She said, "When I see the Sox, I think of you." Well, you'll be doing a lot of thinking over the next week. All good thoughts I pray. Hopefully, you'll pause long enough to put that wonderful smile on display as you think of me as the Sox celebrate on the field. Win it for her.

Win it for Sean, my brother. He and I have shared many days and nights on the phone while watching the games together. Sean knows I tape the games while I'm working (I work nights) so I can watch the games in the morning, but nevertheless Sean HAS to call me at work KNOWING I taped the game to tease me about the outcome. Win it for Sean.

Win it for my mom, another lifelong sufferer. I want her to witness the pure joy that will be shared around Boston, New England and the World. I want her to see one World Series title before it's too late. She will know how truly happy this would make me feel. Win it for my mom.

Win it for Casandra, for she has had to endure a lifetime of me, from the first game I ever took her to in 1988 and especially this year. Back in April—she was completely embarrassed by my yelling at the players at Fenway—to her thoughts as to how humorous it is to see a grown man scream at a TV. To her curiosity as to why I would use a vacation day to watch game 6. She now has a better understanding of the history she has witnessed with me during the Yankee series. She has gone home now. Win it for her.

Win it for that little kid inside me. Win it for my dad for inducting me into Red Sox Nation and the love of the Sox.

Win it for all those past and present who never witnessed a Red Sox World Series Championship. Win it for those in harm's way and especially for those who made the ultimate sacrifice and will never get to see a World Series. Win it for them and their families.

Dad, I hope you, Uncle Leo, Uncle Johnny and Nana will be together up there as you watch the Sox finally win the World Series. Thank you, Dad, for 1967 and a life-long love of the game. I hope you're watching tonight.

—Robert Bransfield

Win it for my father, Bob Holmes. Since I've moved to NYC, I haven't had the opportunity to watch any Red Sox games at all with him, and that's all I ever want to do when I get out of work. He's the greatest father I could ever ask for, and I just want the Red Sox to win just once while he's still around to enjoy it with me.

Thanks.

—Rob Holmes

Win it for my father, Rick Anderson Sr. (1945-1994). My dad lived for the Red Sox. I was his youngest daughter and since my brother didn't come along until seven years after me, I guess my dad got scared he might not get a son, so he decided to make sure he instilled his love of the game into one of us. It worked. Once my brother came along, it became double the fun for my dad.

My dad did it right, too—by the time I was nine years old, he had already taken me to Cooperstown and spring training. He took me out of school on Opening Days—and even caught a foul ball for me one year! He took me out of my third grade classroom to go stand in line at the Harvard Coop the day Roger Clemens had his book signing. He taught me about everything in Fenway, from the retired numbers to the Morse Code. And he succeeded in his goal—I live and die by this team and I wouldn't trade it for anything in the world.

In the ten years that my dad has been gone, not a day goes by that I don't think of him and miss him terribly. But I can honestly say that I have never wished so badly that he were here more than I do right now. My God, how he would love this team. Not just for what they have done, but for how they have done it. With heart, with class, and with sheer joy. Just the way it's supposed to be.

After Game 2 of the ALCS, I had a dream about my dad. I dreamt that I met him at Fenway for a game. We got there early, so early that we were virtually the only ones in the park. We were sitting in the seats that were our very first season tickets, from when I was a child. He was wearing a Red Sox t-shirt, and when I walked up the ramp to our seats and saw him, sitting there all alone in the empty park, he simply smiled and hugged me. I know that it was his way of letting me know that he is here and he is watching. And he is very, very happy.

We still have my dad's season tickets, so I will be at Game 2 on Sunday night. And I know my dad will be there with me.

Please, win this for him.

—Krista L. Anderson

Win it for ....

My father died three weeks ago at the age of 68. Since then, I have felt what I suspect is the usual range of emotions. The sort of sadness that moves me the way the tides move the oceans. An empty nullity of what seems like endless fatigue. But in all that time, not a single tear.

Maybe it's because I have stayed busy. Who knows? It's not as though I took time to dwell on my lack of tears, but it was something I thought about from time to time. Something I thought about the times I held my mother as she cried on my shoulder. Something I thought about when my five-year-old son Liam sobbed one night about a week ago that he was scared that I was going to die. Something I thought about each time I read one of the many thoughtful condolence notes and e-mail messages I received from friends and family.

I lost it Thursday morning, thanks to a message I received from the BoSox list from a guy named Paul Penta:

"I was going to save this for the end of the World Series, but I think the sentiment is valid even now and may help in some way to get us to the promised land.

"This is for….

"All the parents and grandparents, uncles, aunts, cousins, brothers and sisters who took us to our first game at Fenway.

"All of the above who for some reason or other passed on before tonight."

Suddenly I was 7. It was the spring of 1968. The 1967 Red Sox, the "Impossible Dream" team, had captured the hearts of everyone in Boston the previous season. My father agreed to take me to Fenway at the start of the next season. My first Red Sox game.

Thirty-six years after the fact, some of my memories are hazy. I recall clearly that we sat in the grandstand about halfway between first base and the Pesky Pole. I remember being awestruck at the beauty of the field—was that "regular" grass I wondered, or some kind of magical grass? I know the Sox won the game. I seem to recall that Ray Culp was the starting pitcher. I know Ken Harrelson hit a HR. Remember the first time you saw a HR at a game? The arc of the blast was simply astonishing. My eye could not track the ball until I saw it bouncing in the visitor's bullpen. The roar of the crowd was a physical force as we cheered "Hawk" when he rounded the bases.

I don't want to go all "Marcel Proust" on you, but what I remember most vividly were the smells. The cigar smoke. The distant whiff of the green grass. The smell of roasted peanuts and cracker jack (yeah, I had heard the famous song and I wanted everything that went along with being taken out to the ballgame).

And I remember my father putting his arm around my slender shoulders as we left the game, drawing me close to him. Keeping me safe as we made our way through the thicket of the crowd to the subway in Kenmore Square. The faint smell of tobacco and Old Spice aftershave on him. The rough texture of his tweed jacket as it brushed my tender cheek when he held me during the bumpy subway ride home.

We went to many other games at Fenway together over the years. The most notable one was Game 6 of the 1975 World Series, which many consider the greatest baseball game of all time. The Sox that year had had a mail-in lottery for World Series tickets. I sent in the paperwork. About a week later, the postmaster in our hometown, Lincoln, MA, called my mother at home with a quiver in his voice. "You'd better come down to the post office right away," he said, "because I think you are the only family in Lincoln to receive World Series tickets!"

We sat in the CF bleachers on cold aluminum bench seats. Did I mention that it was cold? Bernie Carbo's HR in the 8th inning landed about a dozen rows in front of us. I still think that was my most memorable moment as a Red Sox fan, even though Carlton Fisk, of course, hit his famous walk-off HR an hour or so later.

Thursday morning as I sobbed quietly in my bedroom recalling our trips to Fenway, I flashed back to what I think was the only time my father and I ever played baseball together. We lived in Cambridge then. I might have been 6 or 7. He took me to Cambridge Common, near where the memorial to the Irish famine now sits. I had a yellow wiffle bat. He tossed me pitch after pitch. As I picture the scene, I think my batting stance was all wrong. I "stepped into the bucket" on nearly every swing. I missed many of the pitches. But every once in a while I drove the ball a long way. I would gallop off after the ball, give it back to Dad, and he would throw me some more pitches.

And the afternoons he took off from work to see me play baseball in high school. Since I now have more or less the same job he had then, I can readily appreciate how hard it is to get away from the demands of a busy law practice. I glanced over at a photograph that I have near my dresser. It's not the kind of thing I would have on display on the 1st floor where anyone else would see it. It's a photograph my father took of me playing third base in 1978, wearing the green and white uniform of Concord Academy. That year we won the league championship and progressed into the state quarterfinals. I thought of my teammates, Kevin, Don, and Tommy, and that wonderful team which presumably is still considered the best in our school's history (no matter what Peter Gammons might say to the contrary!).

After all that I have written above, it may come as a surprise to learn that my father disliked sports of all kinds. Maybe it was because he had had polio and had never been able to play any sports himself. I think it's fair to say that each time my father spent time at a baseball game with me was a small sacrifice for him, three hours that I am sure he would have enjoyed more doing something else. But he made those small sacrifices for me and for my sister Kate all the time.

Isn't that the essence of being a good parent? Making small sacrifices. I thought of the day I took my sons to see the execrable movie *Spy Kids 3*, which they had been begging to see for weeks. Liam spent the whole movie running all around the theater disturbing people. Aidan (7) kept asking for popcorn (I agreed), then soda (I agreed with hesitation), then candy (no), then more popcorn (NO!). I thought about the endless games of Pitfall that I and my wife Amy have played with them.

My dad made those kinds of sacrifices. I never thought much about it at the time. I doubt my sons will ever know how loathsome I found those hours watching *Spy Kids 3*. But you do those things to bring your kids a moment of joy. To build a bond. A bond that endures.

My thoughts then turned to baseball and my sons. I took Aidan to his first game at Camden Yards when he was about 6 months old in 1997. A dreary Sunday in May. With a rare good start by Steve Avery (though he never broke 85 MPH on the radar gun the whole day), the Sox won that game. We had "club" seats, which allow you access to a nicely appointed lounge and concession area. While I stood in line to get us some food, Amy sat with Aidan on a sofa nearby. He started to fuss as I was bringing the food over to them and she put him on the carpet for a moment. A small miracle occurred. He rolled over by himself for the first time! It was a scene that I will always remember.

And Liam's first MLB game. A friend had given me his seats for a Phillies game against the Expos. His seats were so close to the dugout on the third base line that you could put your feet on the roof of the dugout. The mascot for the Phils, the "Phillie Phanatic" came by and started playing with Liam. The cameraman caught the action and displayed it on the huge screen in center field.

Liam loved the attention and cooed appropriately until the Phanatic pretended to take a photograph of Liam but shot some silly string at him instead. Liam started bawling so much that the Phanatic came out of character for a moment just to make sure that Liam was OK.

Or the first time that Aidan hit a HR in tee ball. As we drove home from that game, I asked Aidan, "What are you going to tell Mommy about today's game?"

Aidan, who was then only 4 or 5, answered in a way that astonished me. "I want to tell Mommy about my home run, Daddy, but I also want to do something to thank Mommy for all that she does for me. Can we buy her some flowers or cookies to tell her thank you?"

My jaw dropped. I headed to a bakery where we bought brownies. Aidan first presented them to Amy and said he wanted to thank her for being a good mother and only after that did he tell her about his HR about which he was justifiably proud. Let's just say that I think he must get his gift for being considerate from my wife.

My two closest friends who are serious Red Sox fans are named Alan and Jake. For the past 5-7 years, we have shared our love of the Sox (and the Patriots) primarily through e-mail messages. During this magical season and the playoffs so far we have sent each other hundreds of e-mail messages.

After the Sox won in such an amazing way on Sunday, our messages turned to what we call "mojo." The idea, which we will all admit is superstitious, is to try to watch the games after a Sox win in precisely the same way that we watched the win. For example, we were all together at my house for the Patriots' first Super Bowl win, so we insisted on gathering there to watch last year's Super Bowl. On Monday, for example, we agreed that each of us should wear during Game 5 what we were wearing during Game 4's improbable comeback victory.

During Game 4, I had worn a T-shirt that says, "Why Not Us?" on the front and says "Boston 2004—If a nation believes in 25 men, anything can happen" on the back. But I had also worn a plain sweatshirt over it and we all agreed that I had to don both items for Game 5 (I of course continued to wear the same things for Games 6 and 7).

But mojo is about more than clothing. To take my mind off what I thought was going to be the pain of defeat in Game 4, I had worked that night preparing handwritten notes for the people who had sent us condolence cards concerning the death of my father. I had also spent time that night watching the game in bed with my boys when it was time to put them to bed.

So, during Games 5, 6, and 7, I spent time cuddling with my boys in my bed and, after they feel asleep I wrote notes acknowledging the condolence cards. Wednesday night's notes included one to a friend from high school, one to my grandmother, Nana, who is about to be 95 (that note was especially hard to write as you might imagine), and one to a work colleague, thanking him for helping out with work while I was out of the office caring for my father during his final days.

Whenever the Sox got in trouble during the final 4 games, I simply took out my stack of cards and put pen to paper.

Did expressing my gratitude to these people for their support concerning my father's death improve the mojo favoring the Red Sox? Who knows? Obviously, it could not have hurt their chances. Either way, you can appreciate that the Sox success thus far is inexorably tied up for me with both the grief of the loss of my dad, but also the appreciation I feel for their kindness and sympathy.

Thanks for reading this long message. Before I finish, let me return to the idea of small sacrifices. Consider making a small sacrifice of your own. Set aside an afternoon soon to spend with someone you love—a child, a parent, a spouse, a sibling, or a friend. Devote the afternoon to doing something that that person loves to do. Something that might not ordinarily be your cup of tea. Your loved one will appreciate it. And maybe 36 years from now that special person will write to his or her friends and family about what you did in the same way that I just shared with you a memory of something thoughtful that my father did for me in 1968.

Fathers, sons, and baseball. Is it any wonder that many guys will mention *Field of Dreams* on their list of the best movies of all time? Is it any wonder that the MVP of the ALCS was a man whose nickname is Papi?

—Robert M. Elwood

Win it for....

First of all I want to thank all of the people that posted on this thread to make it what it is.

What it did as I sat here reading and tearing up all afternoon was to reconnect me with all the reasons why it has always felt like a special privilege to call myself a lifelong Red Sox fan.

After reading the first 15 pages of this thread, it just came into my head that I needed to call my parents back in Maine. I moved here to Houston a couple months ago for my first "real" job after living with them for a year. We hadn't talked much since I moved, maybe we just needed to get some time away after what was at times a very trying year.

I talked to my mom about her memories, of the Sox, growing up with the generations of her family's Red Sox fans. About her great-grandfather and grandfather and father all who lived in Maine and all passionate about our team. I'd never heard these stories before and I thank all of you for triggering this.

I have wonderful memories of my great-grandparents Mimi and Bumpa, of going over to their house after school to help Bumpa with his garden, and he'd make me a milkshake. I didn't remember, though, about his dedication to the team, or about Mimi's willingness to sit there 162-plus times a year with her husband of 70-plus years. Again, I thank you members of SoSH for helping me to discover these wonderful memories.

So, if you could win it for Bumpa, for Nana and Papa (my grandparents), for all the other members of my mom's side of the family who have lived in and around South Portland as long as there's been a South Portland, and who have lived and died waiting for a moment like what may happen this week.

For my other grandparents, Grammie Bea and Oompa, who I don't call often enough, but I do treasure those summer days up at the lake where the only conversation is the Sox.

Also win it for my Little League coach, who also happens to be my dad, who taught me to play the game, and who I truly sincerely hope is finally on the way to becoming the person we all know he can be. I sat there with him last year for the last game, and here's to new beginnings in life, and to our beloved Red Sox.

Thank you.

—Andrew Rochon

Win it for ....

For my dad, David (1929-1981), who died of cancer without having seen his Sox win the Series. He let me stay up late and watch the '75 WS. For his two brothers,

Allen and Bill, both WWII vets, that didn't see victory either. Allen, who passed away in the summer of 2003, was the last of the brothers. Their father, Allen senior, living in Malden, MA, at the time, did get to enjoy some of those early Sox championships when he wasn't in Europe fighting The Great War. He was a lifelong fan, loved Williams, Pesky, and Yaz. He played ball with the neighborhood kids after work when his sons were growing up in Holden, MA.

I hope that this week his two great grandsons, Hayden and Luke, will be celebrating their first Red Sox victory in Boston. They're 8 and 5 and their dad is letting them stay up late to watch this Series, too.

—Chris Estey

Win it for ....

From 3000 miles away, I'd say win it for every BoSox fan in Britain who breaks out in hives every time they see somewhere wearing an MFY cap as a fashion statement....

.... And win it for Harry and Joe, not yet old enough to understand their old man's obsession, but who will learn one day—probably at the very moment they catch their first sight of the Green Monster and Fenway under lights.

—Mark Smith

Win it for my dad, 10/04/34-4/26/88. He suffered a major heart attack the day before the Bruins finally beat the Canadiens. Not believing he would pass, I told the nurses to keep the TV on so he could see history. He never saw it, but history was made.

To those that suffer similar tragedies this week, I say be strong, you will persevere. History will be made once again. I thought it then, I know it now.

—Jeff Cushing

Win it for my grandmother, who was 12 years old when the Red Sox last won in 1918 and who died last Sept. at the age of 97. I know you're watching and smiling Grams.

Win it for my dad who grew up a Red Sox fan and who died way too young. A huge thank-you for passing on your love of the Sox onto me. Miss you.

Win it for my boys, so that they will never have to go through life listening to the "1918," "Babe," "Bucky," "Boone," etc., taunts.

Win it for every Red Sox fan past, present, and future.

Win it for Tim Wakefield.

—soxgrl3

Win it for my grandfather whom I am named after, Francis Phair, who passed away twelve years ago after watching the many great Sox teams come so close after 1918.

Win it for his wife, Meme, where his passion continues in her to this day. At 94 years young she still watches every game, and was so unbelievably excited when I called her when we finally beat the Yankees it brought me to tears. She passed her love for the Red Sox to me, and I will be grateful for this until the day I die.

Win it for my best friend Louis who passed away early this year in a snowboarding accident. He was a huge Red Sox fan. Every single game he would be in front of the TV first, Budweiser and Red Sox Peanuts in hand. The last he saw of the Red Sox was Aaron Boone, but the childish joy we got that night egging our Yankee fan neighbors house will never be forgotten.

Most of all, win it so my friends and I can believe that somehow this was meant to be, one last meeting between his beloved Red Sox and our Saint Louis.

Make us believe in Destiny.

—Francis Minahan

Win it for ....

My mom who has been fighting off her cancer this year and spends just about every minute of her day taking care of my dad with Alzheimer's. They took me to my first Sox game at Fenway for my 16th birthday and I watched the Sox beat the Yankees and I have never forgotten it. My mom has supported my love for my Sox because she loved her Brooklyn Dodgers and knew what it was all about. We always watched the playoffs and World Series together and she cried with me in '86. What makes this even sweeter is that we both grew up in upstate NY where for every Sox fan there are 10 Yankee fans and she taught me to fight those fans as she did back in the '40s for her Dodgers and now does for our Sox. I'd also like them to win for my newly minted Sox fan nieces so that they never have to know the pain of Bucky ***** Dent, only the joy of Papi. I live in California now with my California-born husband who grew up spending his summers on the Cape. When a friend tried to fix us up after hearing I was from New York, automatically he asked, "Is she a Yankee fan? Cause if she is, I am not interested." We never miss a game, and are very glad we didn't this year.

Win it for my four children…. they have been raised Red Sox fans from the beginning. As the first member of my family to be a Red Sox fan, it was my responsibility to raise them as Red Sox fans. They know the players by name. Some of their first words were "Go Red Sox" and "Yucky Yankees." What they need to know is the feeling of winning now and not having to wait 38 years, like me, for that feeling.

Win it for my wife. God bless her. She had no idea what she was getting into when she married me. She puts up with me watching or listening to every Red Sox game via mlb.com. She puts up with my mood swings when times are tough for the Sox. But most of all, she has become a big fan of the Sox.... she needs to know the thrill of winning.

Win it for me. I cried in 1975 when my sister (a Reds fan) laughed at me. I cried in 1978 when my dad's team (how a New Bedford, MA, boy became a Yankee fan is another story) beat us. I cried in 1986. Worst of all, I cried last year (grown men shouldn't care this much, should they) when I watched a great team, the better team, lose to the most arrogant team in history.

Win it for Red Sox fans everywhere, past and present, who have stayed with the Sox through it all. When it for Pesky. Win it for Ted. Win it for Yaz, El Tiante, Pudge,

and the boys of '75 who through their play, enshrined me in Red Sox Nation for life. Win it for Billy Buckner.

Most of all, win it for yourself. You deserve it. You play the game the right way. You have stayed focused. You have stayed together. You are a TEAM, exactly how I envisioned my Boston Red Sox—the World Champion Boston Red Sox.

—Mike Medeiros

Win it for Squire. My grandfather, Squire, took me to my first Red Sox game in 1978. We sat in obstructed view seats, we found a program to keep score and the game was amazing. Afterwards he bought my first Red Sox hat. I was seven years old and though I moved to California just a year later I was a Red Sox fan for life. Over the years, even when we had little else to talk about, we always had the Sox, which bonded us together. Squire died in the summer of 2001. Born in 1917, he lived through their last World Series, but with no memory of it I had hoped he would live to see a championship.

Win it for my dad. He married into a Red Sox family but grew to support the team and cheered them with me. And when I decided I wanted to pitch in middle school, it was my dad who caught my every pitch. I tried to emulate all my favorite Sox pitchers from Clemens to Hurst to even Oil Can Boyd. We didn't have a catcher's mitt so he just used a poorly padded softball glove and it wasn't till years later I realized how much some of those pitches stung. My dad followed the Sox until his death in the August of 2004.

Win it for my wife. Jennifer always liked baseball but grew up a Padres fan. But marrying me meant supporting the Sox. But she didn't just support the team, she came to LOVE them. Nomar, 'Tek, Nixon, Wakefield, they were her team the way Clemens, Hurst, Rice, Boyd, Boggs and Evans were my players. She got me the MLB TV package so here in Las Vegas, Nevada, we could watch all the games. While the 2003 season once again led to my disappointment she felt it much harder, she had come to LOVE this team. I don't want my wife to ever feel that sadness. She really believed that they would do it in 2003, and she believes again. Win it for Jennifer.

Win it for my son and daughter. Zane is 2 years old and thinks all balls are "baseballs." His first curse words are "Yankees stink!" He is a fan. My daughter, Rian, was just born this summer. Win it for her, let her be born into a year of a championship.

Win it for Jim Rice. He was my favorite player. He was so strong. I remember hearing stories of his great strength. My grandfather swore he was blind as a bat but nothing could ever dim my support for Rice.

Win it for Dwight Evans. Dewey gave his heart to this team.

Win it for Oil Can Boyd. He should have been given the ball in '86.

Win it for Clemens. I know he got the rings with MFY but no matter where he plays he'll always be the Sox pitcher who was the greatest pitcher in 1986.

Win it for Wakefield. He's my kind of pitcher, all heart.

—Cameron Basquiat

Win it for my father, Richard, who made me a fan and has shown me how to keep the faith.

Win it for Maura.... so she can finally wipe away the tears of '86.

Win it for Chris, Becca, and Brian.... my siblings and fellow Sox diehards.

Win it for Billy Bates. He did not get to see the Sox win it in his lifetime, but I know he is smiling now.

Win it for Allison, so that she can grow up as a part of RSN without always having to say…. "Wait till next year."

Win it for Bill Buckner…. It was never his fault.

Most of all win it for everyone who has had their heart broken by the Sox. All they ever wanted was to see them win.

Thank you SOX!

—Gregg Bates

Win it for all those fans who demonstrate that the boundaries of Red Sox Nation are not limited to New England. Those who must survive without 24/7 updates and who are destined to celebrate or comiserate in silence at 4 a.m. when games are shown live. Win it for those who cannot indulge their passion by making regular trips to Fenway, those foreigners who are captivated by the beauty and history of both the park and the franchise and who must cherish memories of Jeff Fassero and Tim Wakefield in a May 2000 game against the Tigers.

Win it for overseas fans everywhere, whether transplanted New Englanders unable to get home, or like this one, devoted "outsiders" who wear the "B" with pride.

—LRedsox
London

Win it for the generations who like me have been born into it, and have never wavered.

…. Alright maybe a little wavering when Haywood Sullivan let Pudge go, and when Lou Gorman botched the handling of the end of Jim Ed's career….

Win it for my mom, who has had to leave the room or turn her view from the TV for the last 35 years whenever an announcer said, "the tying run is at the plate" for the opposition.

Let her stay in the room and watch, and let all of us always expect the best from here on out, no matter what the situation. That transformation has taken place with regards to the Patriots, and now it is the Sox turn.

Win it for my elderly dad who strains to watch games on TV although he can barely see, and always DOES expect the Red Sox to succeed despite decades of disappointments.

We deserve it.

—Guapos ghost

Win it for ....

For my father, who passed away the day pitchers and catchers reported in 2000. Yes, that's how I remember it. For several years before he died we had an annual trip to Pawtucket for Father's Day. When he got sick, we didn't figure it was the end and we bought the tickets anyway. He's got one of them in his pocket, even now.

For my mother-in-law, one of the sweetest women the world has ever known. She loved Tim Wakefield but couldn't watch when he pitched because it hurt too much when things didn't go well.

And win it for my wife who puts up with me when very few people would. I've dragged her all over this country to go to ballgames and she's gone willingly. She hates Roger Clemens with a passion, and Derek Jeter more than anything.

We win this thing, they're getting champagne showers.

—Gregory Lynn

Win it for ....

I don't have a lineage of ancestors who are Sox fans, having never lived in New England, but....

Win this for yourselves—all of you are part of something incredibly special and in one Curt Schilling you have a leader and a force of immense strength and character.

Win this for all the great players I started to follow as a kid in the '70s—for Yaz and Rice and Lynn and Dewey and Pudge (the real one) and Rooster and Remdawg and Eck and El Tiante and for those of more recent vintage—Nomar and Mo and Johnny V and Greenwell and Hurstie and The Can.

Win this for all the great players who preceded me—for Pesky and Doerr and Foxx and Stephens and Rico and Tony C and, of course, The Kid.

Win this for all of RSN who lived their lives and passed away without seeing the Sox reach The Promised Land—including the father of the partner I work for who passed away a few years ago.

Win this for all the kids of RSN, so that they won't have to deal with the cruelty of certain other fans who make caps and shirts with a certain year on them and who worship at the altar of false idols and spells.

Win this for all of SoSH, as you guys and gals are a large part of my Red Sox family—no matter our disagreements on matters political (yes, this means you Pumpsie!) or otherwise we share a bond that is Red Sox baseball.

Win this for all of RSN, particularly those who are serving in the armed forces and for whom tonight provided a huge emotional boost.

And finally, win this for that little kid from Queens who cried in 1978 when Yaz popped out, the teenager who cried when Barrett struck out and the grown man of 34 who cried when Boone hit the ball out—no more tears please, other than tears of joy!!

—Shant H. Chalian

Win it for my father (1913-2000), who was a Phillies fan for years, but eventually started intensively rooting for the Red Sox when I moved to the Boston area many years ago. Mainly, though, he rooted for any team that was playing the Yankees. His passionate hatred for the Yankees was one of the few things that remained when his brain was mostly gone in the last few years of his life.

Win it for my brother's wife, who grew up in Boston, but now lives in the NYC area. Her husband, my brother, is an avid Yankees fan, and for many years she was too, but she has reverted to her childhood allegiance, and would be made very happy by a Red Sox win.

Win it for me. I was born in Brooklyn on the day that the Dodgers lost the WS to the Yankees in Brooklyn in 1941 (the day after Mickey Owen dropped the third strike). I grew up rooting for the Dodgers in my childhood, but their move to LA and my move to Boston cured me of that.

—Patricia Hollander Gross

Win it for the loyal, insanely loyal fans (both past and present) of RSN…. friends/colleagues who aren't privy to the rabidness (is that a word?) of the Nation are constantly being shown examples. Too many personal examples to mention, but here are my favorites the following are true stories....

While in London with a buddy, I of course wore my beloved Sox hat, and as we were exiting Harrods's a fellow member of the Nation give me a wink and a nod. My friend Rob asks, "Dude, do you know that guy?" My response, "I've never seen him before in my life." Rob's comment, "Man, it's like a cult with you guys." Sidenote, Rob experienced the horror last year with me (again starting at 2:00 a.m.), he looks to be on the verge of joining. The boy shows promise as a member of the Nation.

At the opening day of this past Oktoberfest in Munich, I of course, wear my Sox gear, this time the Red Sox Nike windshirt. I mention to another friend and his wife, "Watch, it won't take very long to find another member of the Nation".... mind you this is Munich. I get a "Did you start a little early with the beers?" look. Sure enough, 20 minutes later a U.S. soldier give me a "Go Sox!!" cry during the parade. I wish you could have seen their faces. Sidenote part II, he also shows great promise to join the Nation, sadly she's a Giant fan, but a very good person.

Lastly my thoughts are with those who've lost loved ones who were/are Sox fans (RC etc.).... as I'm sure we've all known another member of the Nation who is no longer around.... for me it was my Granny (the Fresca sipper). And we all know how sweet it will be after the final 4 games. It's a great opportunity to think of those folks and smile ear to ear. I ask you, is there another team or sport that can make an adult man, smile nonstop for a week, the kicker is all day today I just shake my head thinking of my beloved Sox and comment how great these guys are, even when I'm alone (I'm certain people are wondering what's going on).... God, how I love this team. Growing up 3,000 miles from your favorite team can be a challenge, especially pre-satellite and cable TV. I consider myself lucky to have a chance to see them a few times a year at Angel Stadium. I recall many times being asked why I wanted to buy a Red Sox hat/t-shirt etc.... my response: "It's my team."

As has been mentioned many times prior, Shaun, this thread is priceless and should be further documented, You have the makings for a great book here. I'd buy it.... I know most of us would.

—Tony Nielsen
(AnaheimSoxFan)

Win it for ....

I remember the March before last season being a really tough time. The December beforehand my father had been diagnosed with cancer way before his time and given a couple years to live. His health was deteriorating quickly and I was sitting at work seeing that there was a Yanks/Sox ST game televised that afternoon (it may have been the 1st ST game of the year, my memory fails.) I remember saying "@#%$ it" and cutting out of work early—wasn't sure when I'd be able to play hooky to watch the Sox with my father again. So I went to his house and he was in really bad shape; it looked as though he'd lost 100 pounds in that past week alone. He was obviously in a lot of pain but still managed to act incredulous that this new GM kid had Shea Hillenbrand on the block (hey, Dad wasn't perfect). We caught a couple innings and he started to feel really, really bad. I brought him to the hospital and he went that night, dead at 50.

Win it for Mark Passig, the guy who would walk with his son down the block to beehive field to see guys like Clemens, Schilling, Bagwell play for New Britain. Win it for the guy who never had a happier memory than bringing his 6-year-old son to his first Fenway game and seeing Greenwell blast a 1st-inning grand slam with no outs, thus hooking that 6-year-old for life. Win it for the guy who only got to see big Papi as a rock cat, the guy for whom a rookie card for his son was never too pricey, the guy who had the Fisk brawl mentioned in his eulogy. He was a Sox fan for life and so am I.

—Wmjumpstart

Win it for my friend Don Poulin, who passed away earlier this year. Even though he was a Yankee fan, win it for him anyway, as he was one of the first I thought of after the final out last night. We would have given him such a razzing....

We miss you, Donnie.

Win it for all the little ones, who march into the park all wide eyed with their dads or grampas, with glove in hand wearing their favorite Martinez, Ramirez, Schilling, Ortiz, etc., etc., and maybe still even a Garciaparra jersey.

Win it for them so they do not have to endure the years of continuous "Wait till next year" promises as we have had to go through for so many years. Some many more than others.

Yes, win it for the youth of Red Sox Nation.

I wanted to wait for the right time to post this special "Win It For" note. I figured up three games to zip, with one more win to go is probably the perfect time.

Win it for my pal Tim Bell. We were pals since childhood days. But Tim passed away many years ago, much too early. He, like "BoSoxNut" and the rest of the "old gang," was a true Red Sox fan.

I was over Tim's house, with another pal, "Marty," for the 1975 World Series. I vividly remember jumping up and almost going through his ceiling when Carbo hit the game tying home run in Game 6. I was with Tim again for Game 7, when our dream of a Red Sox World Series Championship went for naught.

Tragically, Tim passed a handful of years afterwards.

Well Tim my friend, I'm thinking of you these days. I hope you have HDTV up there.

**—Barry S.
(BoSoxNut)**

Win it for :

My dad, who needs to know it CAN be done.

Ned Martin/Curt Gowdy and everyone that sewed the RS fabric to my soul.

Mike Andrews—we all know why!!!

Yaz who deserves to smile and have a bit of joy for the old towne team.

My brothers, mom, sister and anyone else awakened in middle of night back in '75 by our dad's joy at Fisk's immortal shot.

Every Little Leaguer that gets behind—so they know you can come back from 3-0 (3 outs left) and win it all.

RSN because the job is not done. It's not good enough to just beat the Yankees.

Themselves, the organization and everyone that believed.

My children (T&C) so they can see their dad be happy, joyous and a 10-year-old again!!

New England so we can show the world what it would be like!

The simple reason—Enough is Enough!!!!!

Why Not Us? As long as 25 believe as 1 it WILL be done!!!

Me—so I can confirm my life long belief that TEAM is the answer—Not a curse!

—Geno DiSarcina
(itsareligion)

Win it for my grandfather who passed away on the morning of July 13, 1999, and didn't get to see Pedro dominate the All-Star Game that night. For my father, who has taught me the true meaning of being a Sox fan. And for Rodney, a friend who was tragically taken from us far too early.

—Jeff Goff

Win it for my grandfather, Edward Sullivan, whose perfect day would be on his chair, eating yellow Lays out of the bag, watching his team play ball.

Thank you for the opportunity again and hope you have a great holiday.

—Doug Albert

Win it for my cousin, Wayne Janvrin, who passed. Win it for yourselves and…. WIN IT FOR MY CITY!! Go Boston! Go Sox!

—Michael Valliere

Win it for my family and friends who literally nursed me through testicular cancer. I came through chemotherapy and numerous surgeries and have been clean for over 3 years now.

Win it for my dad, who I was with in the bleachers in '99 for the All-Star Game. I knew Ted Williams was important to him, but saw how much when we both had tears in our eyes as he made his ride around the field. Dad suffered a heart attack on the way to meet me at a Sox game last year. The Sox lost that day, but my dad "won" and was at Games 1 and 2 against the Cards this year.

I've been keeping up with the Sox from Las Vegas, a place I now call home, but I know that my heart is with the Sox and the "Dirty Water" in Boston.

JUST WIN IT!

—David Lazarakis

Win it for ….

Win this for my wife. May her courage as she faces down cancer inspire us all to great things during the time we have. Live today for tomorrow is only a promise. The Sox time is now.

—Matt Audet

Win it for my Danish grandmother, Lucca Lehner, who used to listen to the games in bed while reading Homer's *Iliad* and *Odyssey* in Greek. When games got close, she would turn down the radio almost to the point of silence, just to where she could hear if the crowd roared. Depending on the circumstances—where the game was being played, which team needed something great and shout worthy to happen—she could then tell whether she wanted to enjoy the news now, or give it a night's sleep to steel herself for it.

She caught the fever during the 1975 series and soon became something of an expert. After the last game in 1978, she wrote a letter to the *Globe*, offering her analysis of what had gone wrong. October 10, 1978. The headline is "Olympian Interference":

"Zeus it was who clouded Zimmer's mind and got him to replace that stalwart player Brohamer with Bob Bailey (whom the gods have not loved for a long time). Athena was the one who deflected the ball from George Scott causing him to strike out in the eighth. And later, at that crucial moment in the ninth, she—in the likeness of Don Zimmer—whispered to Burleson the winged words: stay at second!

"So there could not have been any other outcome of this contest. This year. But next year, while forever singing the praises of the glorious deeds of our heroes—Scott throwing a man out at home, Yaz and Evans double-stealing, Fisk fighting off good pitches and Rice sending the ball across the Atlantic—next year we shall at the same time prepare for bringing the embroidered mantles, the golden tankards, the ornamented silver tripods, and the fat hecatombs to Fenway Park on opening day."

And so we shall.

—Adam Lehner

Win it for a boy who lost his mom to cancer back in 1946, whose new stepmother somehow managed to get him a baseball that was signed by all his heroes in the Red Sox '46 starting lineup. Instead of hiding it away, he took it out to the park to play with his friends, because that was the only ball he had, and he just had to play. Win it for my dad, who still regrets losing that ball, somewhere out on the ball field.

Win it for the love of my life, who first noticed me the day I walked into a heated debate he was having with my boss, an Angels fan, about why a Red Sox fan could NEVER root for the Yankees. He turned to me and asked: "Could you ever root for the Yankees?" Stunned by the absurdity of the question, I replied, "What?! You're kidding, right? Of course not. What kind of stupid question is that?" That was the beginning of a beautiful relationship that led to marriage, and today our only regret is that we don't already have children to share this championship with.

Win it for the children we hope to have, so we can tell them this story over and over and over again....

Win it for your wives and loved ones who have stood by you day after day, in the offseason, in spring training, during the long grueling regular season. For all your days apart, for all the calls from hotel rooms, for all the ways they've helped you and supported you as you reach for your dreams. We're so grateful for all they've done for you to help make you the players you are today.

Win it for the first person who ever handed you a baseball. We're so grateful for that person, God bless them.

Win it for your fathers, brothers, and coaches—for all those people who first discerned your talents and gifts, and encouraged you to work, to practice, and to dream. We will thank God for them forever!

Win it for us Red Sox, we've never stopped loving you!

—Susan Despres

Win it for for all those teams who haven't seen a championship in the last 50 years, their players and fans.

Win it for every kid in a Sox shirt, so he or she will not have to endure 86 years of heartache/torment.

Win it for all of the great Red Sox fans who don't read this message board.

Win it for all of the great Red Sox fans who read this message board.

Win it to show everyone that dreams do come true.

**—Mike Espejo
(Sille Skrub)**

Win it for my dad, a U.S. Foreign Service man and a Sox fan who introduced me to the team in 1961. He died in an airplane accident in the Philippines in September 1976, before his time at age 49. His last World Series experience was huddling with 2 friends around a short wave radio in Lima, Peru, cursing first the bad reception on Voice of America and then the outcome of Game 7 versus the Reds.

Win it for my friend and longtime business partner Angus Mountain, a lifelong Sox fan from Dover-Foxcroft, Maine, who passed away from liver cancer this past May at age 50. Last September, a group of his buddies flew with Angus to his last Sox game, a day trip to Camden Yards, where he saw Pedro shut out the Orioles.

Also, win it for all of the Sox heroes who couldn't quite get there, including:

- Johnny, Dom, Bob, and Ted.

- Jim Lonborg, who gave it his all on 2 days' rest in Game 7.

- El Tiante, who threw 163 pitches in Game 4 back in '75.

- Bernie Carbo, who brought us back from the abyss in Game 6.

- The '78 team, for winning 8 straight to force the play-off game.

- RemDawg, who should have had an inside the park home run. I still can't believe Piniella blindly snagged that ball.

- Steamer, who really wanted the ball in the 10th inning of Game 6, and who did his part.

—Tudor Fever

Win it for ....

I married into a Red Sox family, so:

Win the World Series for my wife's mom, for the second time in her lifetime (she was just shy of three months old the last time).

Win it for my wife's dad, who never had it happen while he was alive, although he did see WS games at Fenway in 1967 and 1975. I am so sorry I never got to meet this man.

Win it for my wife, love of my life and best friend, who represented her family at the 1986 WS.

Win it for my wife's brother, season-ticket bleacher creature since the late '80s, who finally gets to see the World Series at Fenway Park.

And win it for my two sons, ages 7 and 4, so they can tell their own grandkids they saw their first game at Fenway the year the Red Sox began winning World Series again.

—Mike Mokrzycki

Win it for all my uncles who've persevered and let a little kid in on all their Sox conversations during family gatherings when I didn't know anything. Truly my favorite part of the holidays.

My two grandmothers who are both Sox fans and have lived through a lot of heartbreak.

My two sisters who rarely complained when our one television was occupied from 7-10 for 7 months of the year.

My mother who has to put up with mood swings from every male in the family during baseball season.

For all the kids out there that would rather sit and watch a 3 hour baseball game than do anything else.

You're not alone!

Lastly, for my dad. He taught me what baseball is really about and made me want to be passionate about a game. He took me to my first game where I can still remember seeing the greenest grass in America for the first time. I used to hope for lots of traffic on the way home so we'd have longer to talk about the game.

Because as much as it was about the game, it was about spending time with him and seeing him having a good time. But most importantly because he's my best friend and it would make his day.

**—Adam Coppinger
(Smokin Joe Wood)**

Win it for my deceased grandfather, Hermon Monroe, who used to sneak into Fenway Park as a kid way back when. His last chance to see the Sox win was in 1986, as he passed away the following year.

Win it for my deceased grandmother, Dorothy Rogers, who always had the radio on the Sox games and the TV on Channel 38.

Win it for my uncle, Lowell Mercier, who has had season tickets since at least the early '70s and witnessed Fisk's HR in 1975 Game 6.... who had tickets to Sunday's Game 4 but could not attend due to emergency gall bladder surgery.... who a week ago told the doctors to operate right away so that he could make it to that game (they did not listen).

Win it for all of my relatives in New England, who still live for this team.... wish I could commiserate with them more often, but it's tough to do from afar.

Win it for my dad, who introduced me to this game and this team, but who I think hasn't connected with the Sox for awhile like he used to but is now coming back to them through my passion.... who is still dealing with the unexpected and painful loss of my mom this past July.

Win it for my five-year-old son, who is not much into baseball but will scream and yell for the Red Sox and boo the Yankees.... who is only allowed to use the words "hate" and "stupid" and the like in the context of the Yankees.... who was the first that I know of to say "Nomar no more" and was sad after the trade, but who really loves to say "Big Papi" now.

Win it for my wife, who must put up with me during baseball season.... who is essentially exiled from watching with me b/c I am such a neurotic mess.... who never even liked baseball before she met me, but who can now quote stats and talk smack to the legions of bandwagon Yankee fans.

Finally, win it for all of Red Sox Nation, so that we can permanently put an end to all the inane "1918" chants, stupid "Curse" talk, and persecution from smug Yankee fans everywhere.

—Scott Monroe

Win it for Red Sox Nation. Through thick and thin we have formed an incredible bond based on community and camraderie, spanning generation after generation. This is what links us—no matter where we live, our age, our status, or our lot in life. Don't ever forget the common bonds, the things we have been through, the memories, the good times, the bad times, the triumphs, the failures, the friendships, the hope that tomorrow is a new day that will turn out will. Never forget the men who have made up this team—those we have cheered, booed, but always admired and rooted for. We are family; and while there are often squabbles; don't forget why we are here and what we stand for. Faith, loyalty, love, hope, tradition....

If this really is the year, don't forget the hope that next year is too.

—Rudy Pemberton

Win it for everyone that's ever rooted for the Sox!

Win it for my dad who introduced me to the Sox.

Win it for my brother, mother, girlfriend and friends who rooted for the Sox; for me, and friends that rooted for them with me.

—Tommy

Win it for my daughter, Becky (who saw her first game at Fenway this year), who kept the faith even when I gave up after 0-3 MFY. She watched every game, always believed, and never gave up. She helped me rediscover my faith....

—Brandon

Win it for my daughter, Joiya. She's nine years old, and watching game 4 with me. They're nine outs away. She has absolutely no doubt in her mind that the Sox are about to win the World Series. The thought of a collapse has never crossed her mind.

May it never.

—Steven Sousa

Win it for ....

I have my mom and dad to thank for my RSN citizenship.... Born in Boston, raised in New Jersey. They protected me from the clutches of the evil empire, and they deserve this one. Thanks, Mom and Dad. Win it for them guys.... God knows they've earned it. Wake, you deserve this more than anyone on that roster. You shut your mouth and go out and play every day, with dignity and respect. A true role model. Have fun tonight!

—Dan Suarez

Win it for ....

I was in college in the mid-'70s. It was a time when my dad and I couldn't talk about anything it seemed, without getting into one kind of argument or another. And yet through all that, my dad and I were still able to talk about baseball, more specifically the Red Sox and the outfield troika of Rice, Lynn and Evans. One of my fondest memories is watching Game 6 of the 1975 World Series with him.

He was scouted by the Red Sox while in high school in northeastern PA, back in the days when Scranton was a Red Sox minor league town. He's been gone 24 years now, but there isn't a day that's gone by that I haven't thought about him…. especially throughout this postseason. I've rooted for the Red Sox all these years in his honor.

This is for you, Dad.

—Jim Monaghan

Win it for my aunt, God rest her soul, who at her funeral, the priest said, "She was a woman of great faith…. She believed she'd see a Red Sox championship in her lifetime."

Win it for my Mom, who's such a diehard fan, and lets me call her and talk stats into her ear for hours. She called me during Game 7 of the ALCS this year when Pedro came in swearing like a sailor, asking why Tito's such a moron. She reads SoSH since I pushed her into it. I was so down after Game 3, I went to go watch Game 4 of the ALCS at her house, and she was so nerved by the game she just went to bed to listen to it there in the 10th, saying if they won to wake her up, but otherwise just let her rest. My sister and I busted into her room screaming that they won on our birthday. She's had a real hard couple of years and nothing would make her happier than having them win.

Win it for my sister, who started watching the Red Sox with as much passion as myself back in 1997, and hasn't stopped. She's braved many Sox/Yanks games in the Toilet bleachers, wearing her Nomar shirt and being called names by those lovely people. She still has her Pedro collage up on her wall from 1999 when Pedro had his 17-K game vs. the Yankees. She's finally understanding why Bellhorn is better, too.

Win it for NJFan who hooked me up with a face-value ticket to the longest postseason game in baseball history and one of the greatest moments of my life (on my birthday, two Sox wins).

Win it for Tim Wakefield, who personifies this Red Sox team. He's a great person, he's the elder statesman on this club, and he does what no one else does, really, in baseball, with the knuckler. He didn't deserve to be the lamb in the Grady game, but he sure pitched with massive balls on Game 5 this year.

Win it for my cousin, who at his wedding, the best man's speech ended with, "Here's to many happy years, many children, and many Red Sox championships."

Win it for my neighbor, who took me to my first Sox game, where I saw the Red Sox win 10-0 over the Royals. I still remember watching George Brett play. He was setting fireworks off with 1 out to go in Game 6 of the '86 series, and I'm sure he won't be doing that this year until it is OVER.

Win it for my old housemates who put up with my antics in last year's playoffs, including basically counselling me through the week after Game 7.

Win it for the college kids who after Game 7, didn't riot, but instead went to the statue of Ted Williams and patted it and yelled, "We're doing this for you, Ted!"

Just win it, please. Do it tonight. I want to cry tonight.

Thanks.

—Ben Cohen

Win it for ....

I've been working abroad since 1988, now living in Shanghai, and I offered the post because I was struck by the way we, although strangers, came together as part of a community around the Red Sox. The thread itself of course illustrated the power of a baseball team to create a community, and this is only a small and undramatic aspect of it, but I had no idea how far-flung it was. And comforting, too.

—Richard Herzfelder

Win it for our Gram (Gertrude Gougeon), who passed away in January 2004. A lifelong Red Sox fan, she was buried with a Sox hat in the same cemetery as Babe Ruth. Though she didn't live long enough to see the Sox win one, we'll always remember her love for the Sox and passion for the game of baseball.

—Cory

Win it for my grandfather, Lawrence "Osty" Ostrander, who died of a heart attack in September 1992. He was a great person who loved watching the Red Sox. He was a sergeant in WWII. He was the most friendly person you could meet and well respected in the community. He passed his passion for the Red Sox on to his son, Richard, who in turn passed it on to me. I hope someday, my son Avery (3) has the same passion.

—John Ostrander

Win it for ....

My mom and I went out to dinner tonight and were talking about how much my dad would have liked to have seen this.

It's funny how life works out—it will be hard to imagine him not being here to see them win. I remember watching the last trip to the WS with him when I was a teenager and thinking even after the loss that they would be back next year, never realizing how long it would be and how much could change in that time.

So, I say win it for Peter Urban Giovanello (1944-90), a Red Sox fan, a great dad, a wonderful husband and someone whose days on this planet were far too few....

**—Sean Giovanllo
(JinHoCho)**

Win it for Paul F. Saint (5/19/1919-11/26/03).

My father.

He was a HUGE Red Sox fan, born shortly after the last World Championship. Died just before this one.

Taught me to love the Sox.

**—Joe Saint
(Saints Rest)**

Win it for my dad 1925-1995, whose last conversation with me was bitching about Ken Ryan blowing a game (7/2/95).

Win it for my mom, 1931-1992, who put up with the family of sports nuts they raised.

Win it for my mother-in-law, who passed in January, just before the Super Bowl, she loved the Pats and Sox.

Win it for us, the true belivers, no front runners here and to be selfish for a moment, win it for this old Moose just once.

—doldmoose34

Win it for ....

I only started lurking at the SoSH about five months ago, and I've never wanted anything posted before. However, the "Win it For" thread ranks among the most meaningful sports writing I have seen. If you could post the following for me, I would be grateful.

My former father-in-law died in July 2001. He grew up in the South End and used to rush to Fenway to be one of the boys who were selected to take people's tickets. He learned some of his greatest lessons in life at Fenway, and he shared them with me often.

By the time I met him, he (like so many others of his generation) refused to have his heart broken any further and pretended to have given up the Red Sox for his hometown Orioles. But his eyes always lit up at the mention of a Red Sox victory, and he still kept a wood block painting of Fenway Park by his easy chair, and somehow, he always knew where the Red Sox were in the standings.

So win it for him, and in his spirit, win it for all those nameless and faceless people who have dedicated their lives (or part of their lives) in order to bring the game to life. To the people in the concession stands, who sell the tickets, who hawk the beer, and who make watching a game possible. And also to those who work behind the scenes, whether it be in accounting or human resources or marketing or the secretaries or the mail clerks—the thousands of people whose names we will never know, who do that which has to be done to keep this great franchise going every year, and who do not get nearly enough credit.

And just win it.

Thanks.

—Alan Sun
(Wade Boggs' Chicken Dinner)

Win it for all of us who dreamed to be Sox players one day, winning the World Series.

Win it for the sleepless and restless, those who stuck through the first 3 games of the ALCS and vowed not to watch Game 4, only to turn on the TV 5 minutes early as always and were glad we did.

Win it for the fans who celebrate alone, for one reason or another.

Win it for Dave Roberts, who while spending most of his time cheering from the dugout, singlehandedly stared down the Yankees and said, "I will score this run."

Win it for the fans in our military, dreaming of Fenway from overseas.

Win it for my wife, who said she hated baseball and my obsession with the Sox, but who had a big grin on her face when Papi won the game in the 12th.

Win it for Manny, who during the strike year of '94 was nice enough to chat up the fans at Fenway, including myself, while a member of the Indians.

Win it for the 3 people who left messages on my cell phone after the win over the Yankees, all of whom I hadn't talked to in at least 6 months.

Win it for this message board, win it for me, win it so I can read on forever about this, my favorite chapter of history.

—Scott Mellon

Win it for my grandfather, Sidney Litner (1919-2003) who took an impressionable kid to watch the greatest hitter who ever lived and endowed him with a passion for life. Papa as I called him spent hours teaching his grandson how to hit the curveball and pore over boxscores on a Sunday morning. In his later years, he lived in Florida and I asked him how it felt to live in South Florida after the Marlins won the World Series. His answer: I may be in Florida, but my baseball heart will always be in Boston. For all of those who passed before us, may your baseball hearts be filled with warmth!

My love for this team started in 1986, the first World Series I remember watching. At that time, I was too young to comprehend what happened in game six. I just remember spreading out my Topps baseball cards, in MN where I have lived my whole life, of all the Red Sox and Mets players before the series and deciding to cheer for the Red Sox because I noticed that Mike Greenwell had the same birthday as I did. That was it, something so simple yet so profound that has led me to share near-ly two decades in the experience we call the Red Sox. Every second has been worth it.

This World Series is for all of you dedicated Red Sox fans who can trump my story (and I know there is a lot of you). You all deserve this! For Scott and Mess, two great guys who made the journey(s) with me to pay homage to this team at Fenway Park over the years. And mostly for my wife, who has embraced this team with me. It has meant so much.

**—Brian Stangl
(dirtdog26)**

Win it for ....

I am one of many thousands that have been brought to the Red Sox by the infectious love and devotion of one of your fans. I live in Vancouver and am an avid Canucks fan. Hockey is usually my flavour. But these last couple of baseball seasons, my friend (Bostonian) has drawn me into the world of baseball. Not just any baseball, RS baseball. And in turn, I have spread this love to my mother, brother and grandmother. I'd like to ask that you win it for your fans whose dedication and enthusiasm has been the inspiration to many new believers worldwide.

"In these days, a man who says a thing cannot be done is quite apt to be interrupted by some *idiot* doing it."
—Elbert Hubbard

The MFYs already feel the effects of this one…. Let's take it all the way boys!!

—Anonymous

Win it for all those who have never seen it, those that hung on so long and just fell short of being able to celebrate it.

Win it for my mom, I grew up in Florida, being the only member of my family not born in Boston, and my mom would check the Red Sox box scores every day and I never even knew she was a baseball fan until 1986, what a time to find out. Win it for her and all those like her that followed the team any way they could.

Win it for Teddy Ballgame and Dom and Johnny, win it for Rico and the Monsta and for Billy and Hendu and Big Jim Ed and all of those that came before.

Win it for Helen B. Robinson 1915-2001 who I am sure is up there with Ted watching every at bat of every game.

Win it for yourselves because you deserve it.

Win it for the biggest party in heaven and on earth.

Win it for us so our children and grandchildren don't have to have another one of these god damn threads!

—SpikeMyOwen

Win it for all the good men and women who wanted to feel this joy and didn't before passing.

Win it for all the good men and women who have invested their hearts in the team for years and who would feel youth and hope and unsurpassed joy at the sight of a Sox victory here.

Win it for everyone in Red Sox Nation who right now is wearing a certain shirt for the fourth straight day or sitting on only a specific spot on the couch or had the same lunch or dinner or who right now has certain sodas or drinks in front of himself. Win it for all these fans who ache at any misfortune the team suffers and who will put themselves through any idiosyncrasy in the hope, however silly or illogical, that there's some inexplicable way that their talisman helps their heroes.

Just win it.

**—James Tetreault
(Rough Carrigan)**

Win it for Sherm Feller, longtime Fenway Park announcer, whose deep voice resonated through you as he announced each batter.

Win it for John Kiley, the late, great organist who entertained millions of Fenway faithful.

—BosoxBob

Win it for ....

FOR DAD (1923-1994)

Started taking me to a lot of games beginning in '77, when I was 8. Although we were living in central NH, we spent a lot of weekends in Boston that year visiting my mother's father, who was in MGH that whole summer. To make it easier on me, we'd go to the park to catch Saturday afternoon games.

After that year, he'd arrange meetings in Boston around the beginning of Sox ticket sales. He'd pick up a bunch of games, then during the summer we'd make the trip down for a weekend series, I'd bring a friend and we'd stay with relatives in the Boston area.

FOR MOM (1929-1997)

She was a hard core fan. Used to tell me about going to ladies day games when she was young, getting in for a dime, etc. etc. She loved Freddy and Dewey during the '70s for both their athletic ability and their looks. She was so bothered when Dewey grew that moustache—I laugh now thinking of what she'd say about this current club's hygiene.

Since Dad was a CPA, it was Mom's duty to take me to opening day every year. From 7th grade through the remainder of high school, I was struck with a mysterious illness that only appeared on opening day. She would drive down every year, navigating by the Citgo sign since she was directionally challenged.

While both parents left me before I turned 30, which is much earlier than they should have, today I've got a warm feeling knowing that they are up in heaven smiling at what this Sox team is about to accomplish.

—Jim Ed Rice in HOF

Win it for .... Yvonne Allain. She cared so much about the Red Sox all of her life and missed seeing the Sox win it all by 5 months, passing away at age 80 in May of 2004. I believe her love for the Red Sox helped her battle through her health problems during those last few years and I hope that someone got the message to her in heaven that "those bums" finally won it all.

—Bryan Allain

Win it for John Miller, who took his toddler son to multiple games a year, and even woke a six-year-old up to watch the '75 World Series, until he passed in a car crash in 1976. He taught me that hating the Yankees is almost as important as loving the Sox.

Win it for Pat Knight, an aunt who picked up the game-attending slack, even letting her nephew miss school so they could attend the 1978 1-game playoff, who lost a battle with brain cancer in 1987 before seeing the team get to this point.

—Dean Miller

Win it for my mom. The person who taught me how to be a Sox fan and never give up hope.

In a bizarre twist of role reversals (not seen in our home since), it was my mom who told my brother and I to wait out Game Five of the 1986 ALCS, while my father wanted us to come to the table and eat the steaks he cooked. Dave Henderson rewarded our faith with a homer tastier than any steak I've ever had and my mother is the one who started it all.

I remember watching my mom cry when we watched the 1986 Red Sox highlight video in February and coming to the World Series part. I want to laugh with her when we watch the 2004 Red Sox highlight DVD in February and come to the World Series part.

Thanks Mom.

—Byron Magrane
(John Marzano Olympic Hero)

Win it for the Petricca brothers who came to Boston from Italy in 1918 and adopted this team and sport as their own but never did get to see the Red Sox win a World Series.

Win it for all of Red Sox Nation.

—Cory Krantz

Win it for ....

I can't do this topic justice but bear with me....

As a young kid coming up the ramp inside Fenway you see that grass for the first time. For me it was religious. For every kid who has walked up those ramps and experienced the heartbreak—win it for them.

For every kid who cheered and cried from afar.

For every kid who who might have a serious health problem and realizes that it's just a game.... Win it for them.

Win it so that somewhere above the aunts and uncles that shared my passion for baseball and the Red Sox will smile.... and that includes the ones on the dark side of this baseball border. Arguing with uncles in '78 about the strength of the Sox with their number 9 hitter smacking 30 homers.... and then having to face the music when Dent hit that ball. Win it.

Win it for my Uncle Chick. Summers spent camping two weeks at a time with his wife, 6 daughters, and one nephew (obviously me). Chopping wood, swimming, those pan sized blueberry pancakes, and sitting in front of the fire with the radio on…. the only "outside contact" we had when camping was the Red Sox game. As soon as it was over, the radio was put away to save the batteries. As other posters have written, we didn't share many words…. but an understanding.

Win it for my mom who called to say, "wow…. what a game" after they took out the Yankees.

Win it for all parents of Sox fans, that there never be even a fleeting thought of "maybe I shouldn't impart my passion for the Sox on them"….

Win it for the members of Sox Nation who are at this very moment serving our country away from their homes—who might otherwise be posting here, or next to us while viewing the game, win it for them.

Finally, win it for Roger Miller of Bristol, CT. Not much of a baseball fan really, but a damned good friend. When I got the call earlier this year that he had died it shook me to the core…. my best friend in college. After years of being laughed at when the Dallas Cowboys were mired in the bad years…. the 1-15 year, etc…. When the phone rang the day after they won their first Super Bowl in the '90s, it was Roger to congratulate me— knowing how much it meant to me. He didn't care who won, but he knew I did, and that is what made him

Roger. My biggest regret is that when the last out is recorded, that Roger won't be able to make the phone ring. Not that his world would be changed, but because he knew mine will be—he'd have called. I have to believe that somewhere above he is happy and smiling, sharing my joy in some way. Win it for Roger.

**—Dewey Schramm
(RetractableRoof)**

Win it for my grandfather, Bob Hooker, who lasted through the Second World War as a POW in Germany but never got the chance to see the Sox win the big one. He always had a positive outlook on life and on the Boston sporting scene in general.

My grandfather was a true student of the game, always keeping up on the *Baseball Encyclopedia* and staying aware of what the Red Sox were doing. Despite going through all the heartbreak over the years, he was always convinced that this was THE year.

I remember from very early on in my life taking trips to my grandparents' house to use their swimming pool. Aside from being able to stay cool on those hot July days, it was always a nice break to spend time with them and catch the Red Sox games on TV38 during the weekend.

Whenever I would leave their house, he would always stand up, shake my hand while looking me right in the eye and leave me with, "Good luck to you and the Boston Red Sox."

My grandfather passed a few years ago but I know that he is resting easy now that the Red Sox have finally won the World Series.

—Todd Duquette

Win it for ....

Win for my sister, who is never without Red Sox gear, and shouting no matter what's happening.

Win for my mom, so she can finally stop blaming Pedro for everything.

Win for the SoSH members, who gave me a deeper appreciation for the greatness of this team and game than I could have ever imagined.

Win for my friend Dan, whose devotion to this team inspired me to keep the faith through thick and thin.

Win for my girlfriend, who one year ago thought we were playing the Yankees in the World Series, and now shows more heart and knowledge than a lot of people I know.

**—Eli Badra
(MIlesTeg)**

Win it for .... my Gram Hurd.... she was born in 1919 (making her 85).... she deserves to see a Sox title in her lifetime.... and I hope that this is the year.

**—Grant E.
(PTiger06)**

Win it for Yo. We had a 14-game lead until he attended his last game at Fenway in 1978. His son, my father, who took him to that game, acknowledged that Yo never did see the Red Sox win the World Series when he delivered his eulogy 12 years ago.

Win it for Stephen Hurricane Smith, a Red Sox fan, who was diagnosed with ALS a few years ago.

Win it for Eloise, who was a year old the last time they won, who took her three oldest children to see Ted Williams' last game, who was so proud of him for not tipping his cap. She proudly wears her BoSox cap surrounded by Yankee fans in Stamford, CT.

Win it for Spalding, a lifelong Red Sox fan and bad influence in the very best sort of way, who never stops believing, even when we're down 0-3.

Win it for Deb, who reports what the Red Sox did, what the Yankees did, what the standings are and how she feels about it every camp morning during dining hall announcements.

Win it for the guy who forgot to bring his Sox hat to Everest whose teammates let me know he'd buy mine off me as I passed them on my way down from reaching my goal at Advance Base Camp (21,500 feet) last April.

Win it for every Red Sox blogger and every last one of the members of SoSH, whose faith and humor helped me get through last fall and winter, and whom I will adore forever for keeping me connected to the Nation from way out here in Seattle. You're living proof that there are no better fans in baseball. Let's go Red Sox!!!

—Jennifer Mahan & Liz Lyman

Win it for my friend Lisa Mitchelson, who succumbed to pancreatic cancer Wednesday, October 20, 2004, at the age of 42. A lifelong Red Sox fan and resident of Hingham, MA, the Sox were a central part of her life until the very end, attending a game with her cousin Kathleen Joyce just a few weeks before she passed away. They joy that I am feeling watching the Red Sox march to the World Series is tempered by our loss, but also providing hope that she is somehow able to see this. I am sorry she can't be here to see this. Win it for her and all others who can't be here.

—J.R. Flanders

Win it for my long lost friend Peter Zonis with whom I spent every game in the bleachers during the summer of '75. I got on the train at Riverside and he jumped on at Newton

Center. What a summer! Win it for my mom, Robin Wallace, who, trying to fill a void when my dad left home, learned how to play catch. Her whacky insomnia is allowing her to watch every game until the final pitch. Win it for my grandfather, Marty Sperber, my link to the 1918 series. He was a huge fan until he died in 1984. We always talked baseball when I visited him in those last 10 years. He loved to razz the umps: "You bum, Neudecker!"

Win it for my Uncle Roger who has an American League body, but a National League soul. Win it for Yaz. As a Little Leaguer in '67, Yaz turned me on to baseball with the greatest season I've ever seen. I can recite "The Impossible Dream" by heart. My Sox have been wicked red ever since. Win it for El Tiante.... I can't pitch to my kids without the kick and the head. Win it for New England.... The home of the most knowledgeable fans in the world. Isn't it a pleasure to be amongst the most passionate and discerning fandom in sports? Win it for my dad, Larry Sperber, who is my personal hero. He has taught me everything about being a man: winning and losing, honesty and integrity. He worked so hard, but always had time to throw it around the backyard. Baseball was a game and family a commitment. His dad took him to the ballgame every Saturday, he took me, and now I'm taking my son. It's wonderful to see baseball through the eyes of your kids. And win it for my best friend, my brother Jimmy. We have been through every season of every Boston sports team for 45 years. No matter where we are, we "Weeeee" each other by phone on every great play, missed opportunity and after every win. We're ATT's dream come true because we don't live in the same area any longer. It's been a long road, Iggy. WEEEEEEEEE!!!

—John Sperber

Win it for ....

Please win it for....

All of yourselves, and all who have gone before you.

My children, so they can live in a better world than the one in which I have grown up.

The members and lurkers at SoSH, all of whom have their roles, just like the Red Sox have their roles, and all of whom make valuable contributions in their own way.

Curt Gowdy, Ken Coleman, Ned Martin, Jon Miller, Joe and Jerry, RemDawg, Sean, Donnie O. and all of the other broadcasters who have brought us every pitch of every game throughout the years.

And all who believe in miracles.

My father-in-law, now in a nursing home because of the terible Alzheimer's that has robbed him and his family of his mind, who took his only child (my wife) to her first Red Sox game on October 1, 1967.

—yazisgod

Win it for my father-in-law.... George Powers.... born December 10, 1920, and passed away October 14, 2004, in Northampton.... when the Sox were down two games to none to the Yanks in the ALCS.... he never saw the Sox record comeback in that series nor a World Championship in his 83 plus years. He had to experience 83 of the 85 years since the Sox last won it all. George was a retired lieutenant detective with the Mass State Police.... my take was that he passed into heaven to solve the curse and straighten out The Babe.... until my co-workers reminded me of Babe's lifestyle and that The Babe was probably in a warmer place.... I still think.... and always will.... that it was George who reversed the curse.... Go Sox!"

—Keith Michaud

Win it for my wife's uncle, Dr. John Molloy. When Carlton Fisk destroyed his knee in 1974, Dr. John led the team of doctors to reconstruct it. We all know what happened in the fall of 1975.

Dr John passed away this summer after a long battle with lung cancer. Win it for him, his children (Jim Jay Michael and Julie) and all of his grandchildren. Win it so they can remember 2004 in a more uplifting and memorable fashion.

—kaspend

Win it for my grandma who would sit and watch Dewey play and proclaim him the best right fielder in the game every 15 minutes, and come to my Little League games faithfully.

Win it for my mother who has lived and died with her husband and family every year the Sox play.

Win it for my brother and sister who faithfully follow the Sox, regardless of where they are. My brother was in England last year when the MFY pulled their crap and won. His email to me was simple, yet painful, It said all that needed to be said for a member of the Nation.

Win it for my best friend, Paul, who lives in Somerville with his wonderful wife, and has prayed for this day with me since we were 7 years old.

Win this for my beautiful fiancée, who after one trip to Fenway last summer became a Sox fan, and who has tolerated and supported every thing I have done when the Sox play.

Most of all, win this for my father, Kevin Nolan Sr., a man who brought me up to live and die by the Sox. The man who brought me to Fenway when I was 6, and bought seats right behind home plate, and bought me a souvenir that still sits in my desk (a small, wooden bat with "Boston Red Sox") burned into it. The man who would share stories of seeing Teddy, Doerr, Pesky, and Dom play. The man who sits in his usual chair at his beloved Cape Cod home and tunes into NESN every night during the summer and fall months. The man who engages me in conversation about the Sox within 10 minutes of my seeing him. The man who taught me the virtue of loyalty, and sticking with your team through thick and thin. The man who taught me all my curse words after what happened in '86. The man that has his private parking spot by the Citgo sign that no one else is privy too, and piles up his Fenway Franks with those chopped onions. The man who taught me how to be a RED SOX fan. This is for you, Dad, and everyone else who stayed faithful all through the years. KEEP THE FAITH!

—Kevin Nolan Jr.

Win it for ....

I feel compelled to add my son to the list of children we hope never have to go through what we have all been through in one way or another.

Please win it for Brady, so that he never has to feel inferior to any fan.

Brady is almost 2 now and he has never known anything but the Sox in the ALCS. That's kinda cool but not as cool as what we are all hoping for.

Win it for Red Sox Nation. The most loyal, passionate fan base in the world.

Please please please just win. One More Time.

Why Not Us?

—Mike Furlano

Win it for ....

My wife, Stacia, so she doesn't have to suffer by watching me have a complete breakdown again. She puts up with me staying up late to follow the game threads, and she knows when I need space and when I need someone to jump up and down with when we achieve the unthinkable. She was baptised into RSN last fall and even allows us to raise our 21-month-old daughter, Ashley (who had her first Fenway experience in May) to cheer for the Sox. God bless her!

—PT Sox Fan

Win it for my mother who will not have a chance to see this: Joyce Gray Overton 1942-1989. She took me to see my first Sox game when I was in the first grade around '80-'81. I don't even remember most of the game or who they were playing but I remember the last at bat. Jim Rice was up to bat at the bottom of the ninth with the tying run on base. He struck out swinging but the crowd was behind him every step of the way. I remember her saying to me: "He wanted it so bad." The thing I noticed the most was there was no sadness that day. Everyone in the park knew that Rice wanted that win for us more than for himself. It was that moment that I became a Red Sox fan for life.

—Paul Clinton

Win it for my dad and my grandpa, with whom I share my name. My grandpa, because he is 94 and was too young to really remember the last time we won. At this point, he is in a home, and the only things that really keep him going at this point are the Sox and the large-print westerns he reads over and over again. Despite the fact that he sometimes doesn't remember my name, he always seems to know what's going on with the Sox, and he has been waiting a long time for this. I've been hoping for the last 10 years (since his health started declining) that we'd get one before he passed.

And for my father, who started taking me to games in 1982 and who instilled the love of the Sox in me. Despite the fact that he lived in NH and I grew up in NJ, he still took me to several games every summer. It was me and my buddy AJ who were the only Sox fans in my high school, everyone else was Phillies, MFY, or the Mets. But Dad raised me right.

—Flailing Jerry

Win it for every Mom or Dad who bought the Red Sox yearbook for their kid every year because they knew every page would be memorized by the end of April.

Win it for my grandfather who is responsible for one of my first words being "Boom-ah."

Win for every great player who never quite got there.... Yaz, Dewey, Rice, Remy, Greenwell, Nomar.... and all the fans we wish could be here right now.

Win it for every kid that wore their favorite player's number in Little League and dreamed of being on the field when we finally won it. (I wore Remy, and Spike Owen when I grew out of #2)

Win it for my wife, Emily. She got introduced to this craziness with a phantom tag in '99, got punched in the stomach in '03, and witnessed everything that is good about sportmanship, teamwork, and friendship in '04.

Finally, win it for all of us idiots that live and die with this team and understand that it is bigger than just a game.

For my dad, Robert J. Hardy, who recently passed. Some of my fondest memories are linked to baseball and watching the Red Sox in particular. He was the man who took me to my first Sox game as a toddler, taught me how to throw an overhand curve as a teenager, and made me into the man I am today. Dad passed away from cancer in August of 2004. Remarkably, his first operation was the day after Aaron Boone's home run landed in the left field stands at Yankee Stadium. I was overwhelmed with emotion after Game 7 of the ALCS because I had always called Dad after Sox games. Like a typical fan, he always had plenty to say after wins, and even more insight after losses. It sucks that he's not around to enjoy this historic postseason, but part of me can't help thinking he's up there with the Big Guy watching it all unfold.

—Ryan Hardy

Win it for Frank "Sam" Duham Jr., my grandfather, who taught me everything I know about being a Red Sox fan, and volumes more about being a man. He was born in 1918, died in 1998 and never saw it happen. I will always remember Sam bending down to say goodbye to me at his home when I was five years old and wearing a Yankees hat my mother had put on me. Sam leaned down and said, "Just so you know we don't let Yankee fans in this house." I spent the entire car ride back to my house peeling the letters off that hat. I love you Sam!

—Stephen A. Smith

Win it for Clear's Cleaver, who has watched 7 games this season with his 3-week-old son, James. Need I tell you which 7 games they were?

Yes, Clear's Cleaver, with whom I watched some great and some painful games in 1986; with whom I walked the halls of Cheshire High School in Sox jerseys following the '86 Series, prompting even the most obnoxious MFY and Met fans to say "classy fans, guys."

Yes, Clear's Cleaver, who once, to my chagrin, prematurely declared the Sox World Champions and who has lived to hear about from me for the last 18 years. Free him from his sin once and for all. Let him make the declaration again this year, and let it ring true.

Yes, Clear's Cleaver, who introduced me to the Sons of Sam Horn. Thank you, brother.

—Sean

Win it for Mimi who would go to Sox games in the '40s while she was in nursing school and Grandpa was in the war.

Win it for my dad who is 8 hours away but "watches" the game via telephone after every amazing play.

Win it for my best friend Greg who has had season tickets since I have known him, and for his father and granfather who have had Sox season tickets since long before that. Win it for my boyfriend Brian whom I dragged to PA and is not able to enjoy the games in New Hampshire.

And win it for my friend Jake, who passed away 9/29/04 at the age of 23 and whose wonderful spirit is helping the Sox along as much as it can.

Thank you for doing this for all the Red Sox fans out there.

—Danielle L. Richey

I have been a lurker for 2 years now. I feel like part of the family although only from the outside. Consider me your next door neighbor. I grew up in VT and live in Boston now. My father brought me to Fenway for the first time in '75 when I was five. My father was in the bleachers during the Series in '67 and saw the Sox lose. My father and I went to Game 3 in '86 and saw the Sox lose when the *Globe* had a cover story that day about the dark clouds lifting above Fenway. I cried in '86 and felt like a family member died in '03. My father and I returned to Fenway this Sunday to see the Sox win Game 2. Win it for my dad, a great man and a great father. Win it for his father, my grandfather, who died before the Sox

could win it and was buried with a baseball. Finally, win it for my two sons, so they can root for the Sox without all the baggage.

—Sam

Win it for Victoria Snelgrove. What a shame something so tragic had to come from this remarkable season. May her family find peace in their hearts.

Win it for the baseball fans in the military who can't be here in person to witness history. Thank you for your service.

Win it for the diehards on SoSH. Your passion is unmistakeable and is one of the reasons players like Schilling are willing to play for our team.

Win it for the 2004 Red Sox. Thank you for the highs and lows of the past two seasons. Your unwillingness to give up will provide inspiration forever.

Go Sox! Let's finish this!

—Daryle

Win it for my mom who was sick with cancer during the last Sox World Series. Even as she lay ill, she insisted I watch the Series to lift my spirits as a young boy back then. Win it for all the times she drove me to see the Red Sox play in Chicago at Comiskey, and the times she drove me to Milwaukee the next day because I hadn't yet gotten my

Red Sox fix. And win it for my dad, who after all of our years of a strained relationship, still finds time to talk about baseball. When I talked to him in the hospital just days ago, we basked in the Sox triumph over the Yankees in the ALCS. Win it for every parent who shielded their child from the realities of life so that we could live in the world of baseball for just one day longer....

—E. Wolfgang Niedert

Win it for Lena Marchetti, my mom, born in 1919. Mom was a very strict Italian Catholic woman. The only time I ever heard her curse was when the Sox were on. I would come home from school and she would be ironing with either the radio or TV on. If the Sox were winning, she would say, "That's my boys!!!" as if she raised them all from infancy. If they were losing, she would shout "Dammit Sox, dammit!!!" Yup, that was the extent of her cursing.

She loved Ted Williams and Johnny Pesky. They were gods to her. She could quote batting averages and pitchers' ERAs in a way that would make Eric Van proud. She taught me the infield fly rule.

My middle daughter lives in Middleboro now. She called me yesterday to tell me that she bought an AL pennant and placed in on my mother's grave. She promised to be back with a World Series pennant.

Win if for Lena Marchetti. She always kept the faith.

—Linda Lane

Win it for all of us—the diehard Sox fans who have lived and died with this team for years, who despite all the close calls, near misses, and heartbreaks, still root, still wear the Sox hat everywhere we go, and wouldn't root for another team, or stop caring about this team no matter what.

Win it for all the Sox players past and present who are someplace rooting for the Sox to get it done.

Win it for Pedro, the greatest pitcher I have ever watched. When he was at the top, there was nothing like a Pedro start at Fenway Park. I'll never forget 17 Ks one-hit at Yankee Stadium, game five against the Indians, game three against the Yanks, Pedro-Clemens in New York, and on and on.

Win it for Manny, who was all but run out of town, put on irrevocable waivers, and came back, and just played this year. As Peter Gammons said, is he a perfect player, no, but he just plays.

Win it for Schilling. He just gets what it means to play in Boston, for Boston.

Win it for everyone on this team. The ride this team has given us not just the last few weeks, but all season, has been something I will never forget.

Win it so I never have to hear about collapses in terms of the Red Sox, so I don't have to hear about 1918, Babe Ruth, Bucky Dent or Aaron Boone.

Win it to get Bill Buckner off the hook, as I can't believe how many people don't know the game was tied at that point.

Win it for my brother. Anytime I think I have gone insane with how I follow this team, I think of him, and realize I have a long way to go until I cross the line into complete insanity. I cried because you cried after game 6 in '86—hopefully we get to cry again for the right reasons, and I wish I could be there to watch the game with you.

—Ben Miller

Win it for my mother, and all mothers like her out there, who watches these games not because she loves baseball, but because she loves her sons and wants to know how her sons are, and the mood they will be in.

Win it for my father. A man who got along with everyone, liked everyone, and hated the New York Yankees and hated Yankee fans. A few months before he passed away, we went to a Yankee-Sox game, and it is a day I will never forget for no other reason than I got to spend a day at Fenway with my dad. He didn't get to see it, but as much as anyone, he would have loved watching the Sox this year.

Lastly, just win.

Thank you. Thank you 2004 Sox. Thank you for winning it for everyone in Red Sox Nation, for people who've endured for 86 years. Thank you, personally, for winning for this man who's crying tears of joy the other side of the world. Thank you.

—Daryl Sng (singaporesoxfan)